About this book...4

About this book

CityPack Beijing is divided into six sections to cover the six most important aspects of your visit to Beijing. It includes:

- The author's view of the city and its people
- Itineraries, a walk, a cycle ride and excursions
- The top 25 sights to visit – as selected by the author
- Features about different aspects of the city that make it special
- Detailed listings of restaurants, hotels, shops and nightlife
- Practical information

In addition, easy-to-read side panels provide fascinating extra facts and snippets, highlights of places to visit and invaluable practical advice.

CROSS-REFERENCES

To help you make the most of your visit, cross-references, indicated by ▶ , show you where to find additional information about a place or subject.

MAPS

- **The fold-out map** in the wallet at the back of the book is a comprehensive street plan of Beijing. All the map references given in the book refer to this map. For example, the Hall of Supreme Harmony in the Forbidden City has the following information: 🗺 **G6** – indicating the grid square of the map in which the Hall of Supreme Harmony will be found.
- **The city-centre maps** found on the inside front and back covers of the book itself are for quick reference. They show the Top 25 Sights, described on pages 24–48, which are clearly plotted by number (**❶** – **㉕** , not page number) from west to east.

PRICES

Where appropriate, an indication of the cost of an establishment is given by **£** signs: **£££** denotes higher prices, **££** denotes average prices, while **£** denotes lower charges.

CityPack
Beijing

SEAN SHEEHAN

Sean Sheehan lived in south-east Asia for eight years and travelled extensively in China, first visiting the country in 1986 by taking a slow boat from Hong Kong to Shanghai with his two children, then aged four and six. Sean Sheehan is also the author of CityPack Hong Kong. *When he is not travelling, Sean lives in West Cork, Ireland, pursuing his interests in beekeeping and the countryside.*

City-centre map continues on inside back cover

AA Publishing

Contents

BEIJING
life

A PERSONAL VIEW

A word of advice

Beijing is a fast-changing city in many ways: visitors should be aware that hotels, restaurants, clubs and bars can close, move or change name more rapidly than in most cities. In addition, few people speak English, except in tourist hotels. If you wish to visit any establishment listed in this guide, you are advised to ask a member of staff at your hotel to telephone and check that it is still open and at the same address. The same person can then make a reservation on your behalf if necessary.

All cities develop and change, but what is happening in Beijing is astonishing. A visit to Beijing in the 1980s was hard work but Beijing is a very different city today. All the troublesome aspects of a visit back then have faded into the background – to be replaced by the fun of exploring one of the world's greatest capitals. You no longer need special certificates to go shopping; the difficulty of even finding a store to make a simple purchase of fresh fruit or aspirin is now a quaint memory. Buses are impossibly overcrowded still, but inexpensive taxis are commonplace and finding your way around is more straightforward. In the old days even finding a decent place to eat could be a challenge.

Beijing, chosen in 1260 by Kublai Khan as his winter residence, and now capital to a nation of over one billion people, is undergoing profound changes. Anyone spending time in the city has the unique experience of being able to observe a social revolution every bit as radical as Mao Zedong's 1960s Cultural Revolution. Visitors will still encounter old Beijing even on main thoroughfares: a bicycle repairer squats on a street corner with his tools, waiting for a passing cyclist with a puncture; down an adjoining *hutong* (alley or lane) people still insulate the walls of their homes with newspaper. But evidence of a new society is everywhere. Beijingers are embracing

Consumerism has arrived in Beijing

consumerism with revolutionary fervour. Signs and menus appear in English, mobile phones are commonplace, nappies on toddlers are replacing trouser flaps. The people of Beijing are sampling what the West has to offer and observing the process is enthralling.

Despite these changes, it is China's 3,000-year-old civilisation that remains at the heart of Beijing's appeal. During over 800 years the city has been home to 33 emperors of four great dynasties, whose rich legacy includes such major sites as the Forbidden City and the Great Wall. More recent triumphs and tragedies are enshrined in Tian'anmen Square. Visitors can also experience China's ancient culture in more living forms: restaurants specialising in regional cuisines open a window on one of the world's most incredible food cultures; traditional tea-houses are reopening; Chinese opera is back in favour, and every evening a theatre plays host to the 2000-year-old tradition of acrobatics. What prompted the early waves of independent travellers in the 1980s was the expectation of seeing all of this and experiencing at first hand a culture that had shunned the West. This is still the chief draw, but now it can be enjoyed with the benefit of creature comforts, and is made even more astonishing by the city's social renaissance. Beijing has flung its doors wide open. Go in.

Past and future

One night from a bus window in the heart of the city a small group of elderly citizens could be seen gazing up with sceptical awe at a glistening chrome and glass tower block whose flashing neon broadcast the name of a familiar Japanese camera company. These men and women could have witnessed the founding of the People's Republic in 1949 and they definitely survived the tumult of the Cultural Revolution. What are they thinking now?.

The older generation has witnessed another revolution

EVERYDAY BEIJING

'Early to bed and early to rise' is as true of Beijing today as in imperial times, when giant bells rang out the hour of dawn from the towers of the Forbidden City. In the days of Mao Zedong every home had an alarm clock painted with a revolutionary theme (they can be picked up for a few pounds from enterprising vendors) and people woke up ideologically fit for a hard day's labour. Beijingers nowadays still rise with the sun and if you do too, then you should visit the public park nearest your hotel one morning, before 8AM, to see Beijingers of all ages performing tai chi. This Chinese form of calisthenics is spiritual in nature (➤ 52), as opposed to the modern dancing sessions that also take place early in the morning as a form of physical exercise. One consequence of most Beijingers making an early start is that lunch happens around noon and evening meals are over by 6:30. Time must be allowed for housework, for there are no housewives; and do not be fooled by the presence of familiar advertisements for household appliances: most homes do not have washing machines, vacuum cleaners or the like.

Early morning dance in Tiantan Park

Family survey

The average income for an urban family in China is 14,000 yuan, according to a 1997 survey. For Beijingers the figure is likely to be a little higher because of the greater opportunities to work in the private market. The survey also revealed that residents of the capital have the most cash under their mattresses – around 24,000 yuan per family.

Usually, both members of a married couple work each day, and they are likely to have time together only on weekends. Sunday is a day off work for most state employees and, in a city of over 11 million people, that means heavy-duty shopping (for this reason, try sightseeing rather than visiting the shops on Sundays in Beijing if you can).

It is more common for one adult in the family to leave state employment and work for a private enterprise – perhaps in a hotel – while the other stays within the state system for security. But for how long? They have heard the stories of massive unemployment in state industries outside the capital, and feel they are lucky to have a job.

BEIJING IN FIGURES

THE PLACE

- Beijing's total area is nearly 17,000 sq km, roughly that of Belgium. The city limits (including rural areas) extend for 80km
- The city is one of the few world capitals not situated on a coast or navigable river
- Beijing is roughly on the same latitude as Rome, Madrid and Philadelphia

THE PEOPLE

- Beijing is home to 1 in 100 Chinese people
- The official population exceeds 11 million
- All of China's 56 nationalities are represented in Beijing, but the Han people account for over 96 per cent of the city's population
- The Chinese language is a series of dialects, mutually incomprehensible to the ear even though they share a common set of characters. To facilitate communication between Chinese from different regions, the dialect of Beijing has emerged as the basis for a common spoken language. Known as Mandarin, *putonghua* to the Chinese, it is learned by non-Beijingers as a second language

Chinese characters are difficult to master but street signs are romanized

SURPRISES

- A 1995 municipal law decrees that no dog taller than 35cm can be legally raised in Beijing
- During the 1995 UN Women's Conference, a temporary law, now rescinded, was enacted forbidding residents to hang laundry from windows
- "So great a number of houses and of people, no man could tell the number…" What Marco Polo observed in the 13th century still seems true today
- Beijing's railway station can hold up to 14,000 people on its platforms – more than any other railway station in the world
- Some 9 million bikes are pressed into service each morning across the city. In a sign of changing times, bicycle thefts have jumped by 700 percent in recent years, and in 1996 some 80,000 were stolen

9

A Chronology

700BC	Mongols, Koreans and local Chinese conduct trade where the capital is now located, and its position on the southern edge of the North China Plain attracts military leaders.
AD1215	Mongol warrior Genghis Khan captures a small town called Youzhou (Tranquil City) and his grandson Kublai establishes his capital in the renamed Dadu (Great Capital) by the end of the century. Marco Polo is astonished at the wealth derived from its position at the start of the Silk Road.
1368	The Mongols are defeated and the Ming dynasty established. The capital moves south to Nanjing but the second Ming emperor returns and, building the Forbidden City and the Temple of Heaven (Tiantan), becomes the great architect of Beijing.
1644	The Manchus establish the Qing dynasty and develop and expand the capital over the next century. The great Summer Palace is laid out and built north of the city.
1860	Anglo-French troops attack Beijing and burn the Summer Palace during the Opium Wars. In 1884 Dowager Cixi misappropriates funds earmarked for the navy and orders the building of a new Summer Palace. Hermetically sealed within the Forbidden City, she is cut off from the real world and oblivious to the poverty and discontent that is spreading through the country.
1911	Successive waves of occupation by foreign troops weaken the imperial order and the Manchus are overthrown. The Nationalist Party takes power and the Republic of China is established with Sun Yat Sen as president.
1928	Beijing is under the control of Chiang Kai Shek before falling to the Japanese in 1937. After 1945, following the defeat of the Japanese, the civil war that began in 1927 resumes between Chiang and Mao Zedong's Communists.

1949 In Beijing the victorious Mao announces the People's Republic of China and the remnants of Chiang's Nationalists flee to Taiwan. Soviet experts help the Chinese tear down and rebuild large parts of Beijing.

1966 Beijing is the scene for the start of the Cultural Revolution, Mao's master move in a power struggle within the Communist Party. Red Guards wave their little red books and the country's schools and universities remain closed for a decade.

1976 Mao dies and, soon after, Deng Xiaoping takes power. Westerners are admitted into the country, and special economic zones are created, allowing foreign investment.

1989 Students mass in Tian'anmen Square and demand political liberalisation. The government decides to impose order by calling in the army to disperse the students.

1997 Deng's death leaves Jiang Zemin as paramount leader, and he witnesses the return of Hong Kong to Chinese rule.

1998 Life in Beijing seems stable but there are major economic and political problems as the country deals with the transition to capitalism while retaining one-party rule.

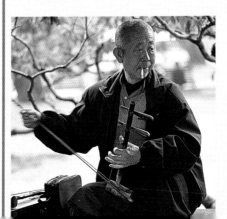

Traditional Chinese music remains popular in this fast-changing culture

PEOPLE & EVENTS FROM HISTORY

Mao's Litttle Red Book was read zealously in the 1960s

EMPEROR YONGLE (ruled 1403–1424) – BEIJING'S ARCHITECT

When Emperor Yongle, (his name means eternal joy) the 26th son of the first Ming emperor, took the reins of the dynasty in 1403, he moved the capital north from Nanjing to the older city of Dadu, strategically closer to the Mongols. At the beginning of the Mong era, Dadu had become Beiping ('northern peace') but Yongle rechristened it Beijing ('northern capital') and called in geomancers to advise on the building of a new imperial palace (the Forbidden City) and a sacrificial temple (Tiantan). Ordinary citizens who were not permitted to enter the Forbidden City set up homes around the walls and the layout of Beijing has remained largely unchanged since the days of Yongle.

EMPRESS DOWAGER CIXI (1834–1908)

Cixi first entered the Forbidden City as a concubine to a Manchu emperor. When he died in 1861 she became regent to their infant son. From then until her death she was the effective ruler of China: a deeply conservative figure who was renowned, among other things, for releasing 10,000 caged birds each year on her birthday. She acquired the nickname 'Old Buddha', and following her son's death chose her nephew to be emperor. When he tried to introduce reforms she had him confined to the palace as a virtual prisoner. The day before she herself died she organised his murder.

MAO ZEDONG (1893–1976)

The son of a well-to-do farmer in the Hunan province, Mao adapted Marxism to suit rural China. When his fellow communists were threatened by Chiang Kai Shek he organised the famous year-long, 9500km Long March across 18 mountain ranges and 24 rivers to escape capture. After he proclaimed the People's Republic in 1949 his policies dominated Chinese life until 1976 Despite official acknowledgement that Mao made some mistakes, he remains a deeply revered figure amongst the older Chinese and his influence continues to be felt.

BEIJING
how to organise your time

13

ITINERARIES

In Beijing planning your time is essential, especially if it's limited. You really need at least three days, but a longer stay which allows time not only for seeing some of the major sites but also for slowing down and observing some aspects of Beijing life is much more worthwhile.

ITINERARY ONE	**THE FORBIDDEN CITY & THE SILK MARKET**
Morning	Start early with a visit to the Forbidden City (➤ 31), entering through Meridian Gate (➤ 51) and leaving by way of Shenwu Gate (➤ 51). If time and energy allow, cross the road outside to visit Jingshan Park (➤ 30).
Afternoon	Go shopping in the Silk Market (➤ 75) and the Friendship Store (➤ 74), a short walk away to the west. Take a taxi or walk further west to Tian'anmen Square (➤ 38) for the flag lowering ceremony at dusk.
Evening	Catch the China Acrobatic Troupe at the Chaoyang Theatre (➤ 82) for an exhilarating evening or stroll along Wangfujing and take in the Forbidden City at night (➤ 18).
ITINERARY TWO	**TIANTAN PARK & SANLITUN**
Morning	Start early enough that you can reach Tiantan Park in time to see Beijingers practising tai chi (➤ 8) before visiting the Qinian Hall (Hall of Prayer for Good Harvests ➤ 44), and the Imperial Vault of Heaven (➤ 45) within the park. Leave by the east gate, passing the Tiantan Market stalls selling cultural curios from the 1960s (➤ 77). Then, if time allows, cross the road to the Hongqiao Market (➤ 73) where pearls, arts and crafts items and antiques are for sale.
Afternoon	Visit the Sanlitun area (➤ 75) for shopping and fit in a reconnaissance of the restaurants (➤ 64–9), bars and clubs (➤ 78–81) for a return visit in the evening.
Evening	Return to Sanlitun.

ITINERARY THREE	THE GREAT WALL
Morning & Afternoon	Join a day-long tour (booked ahead if possible) to the Great Wall (▶ 27) and Ming Tombs (▶ 28). Tours usually include lunch.
Evening	Visit the Beijing Concert Hall for classical Chinese music or take in one of the dinner shows with a Beijing roast duck meal (▶ 82–3).
ITINERARY FOUR	THE SUMMER PALACE
Morning	Visit the Summer Palace (▶ 24), or spend the morning in Tian'anmen Square (▶ 38) visiting the Chairman Mao Memorial Hall (▶ 41) and the Museum of the Chinese Revolution (▶ 43). For something more active, join the masses on two wheels and hire a bicycle for a tour north of the city centre (▶ 17).
Afternoon	Experience the Beijing underground by heading for the Yonghegong (Lama Temple, ▶ 47) or visit the quieter Great Bell Temple (▶ 26).
Evening	Enjoy an evening of cultural entertainment at the Lao She Teahouse (▶ 83) or return to Tian'anmen Square for a stroll through the lonely expanse of Beijing's political heart.

Some of the 9 million bikes used daily in Beijing

WALK

THE SIGHTS

- Lu Xun Museum (➤ 54)
- White Pagoda Temple (➤ 57)
- Guangjisi Temple (➤ 56)

INFORMATION

Distance 1.5km
Time About 2 hours including sights
Start point Opposite Bank of China on Fuchengmennei Dajie
🚇 D5
🚊 Fuchengmen
End point Bank of China on Fuchengmennei Dajie
🚇 D5

OFF THE TOURIST TRAIL

This walk shows workaday life for ordinary Beijingers as they go about their daily business. It also provides an opportunity to visit several lesser-known places of cultural interest that might otherwise be overlooked.

From Fuchengmen underground station walk the short distance to the junction with Fuchengmennei Dajie, cross the road and turn right for the first stop at the Lu Xun museum. (Look for an English sign in blue, pointing the way to a municipal government department, just before a Kentucky Fried Chicken restaurant.) A cobbler and food vendors have stalls down this side street on the left; the museum is at the end. Continue along Fuchengmennei Dajie and look for a shop at No 165 selling medicines. The Nepalese-style White Pagoda Temple, which towers over this section of the street, is reached by turning down the *hutong* (alley) at No 165.

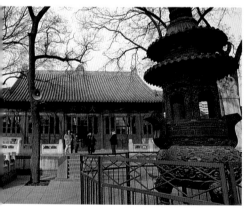

Guangjshi Temple dates from the 12th century

Continue along the main road, passing a high school (which used to be a temple) opposite a large red wall on the other side of the street. Carry straight on across the junction. At No 25 there is the entrance to the Guangjisi Temple. At this point, either retrace your steps, or hop on a No 101, 103 or 42 bus which will take you back to the start point where there are refreshment possibilities. There is an Indian restaurant (➤ 67) in a hotel which also offers an inexpensive lunch buffet serving international cuisine, and an American fast-food restaurant next door. The Vantone New World Shopping Centre (➤ 76) also has a fast-food outlet.

CYCLE RIDE

PARKS & LAKES

A cycle tour gives the satisfying feeling of experiencing an essential aspect of Beijing life. Hire a bicycle from your hotel (most hotels rent bicycles) and always use the cycle lanes.

Head south down Wangfujing Dajie and turn left on to Dongchang'an Jie and left again on to Dongdanbei Dajie. Cycle north up this name-changing road for 4km, almost to the Yonghegong (Lama Temple), near the main junction with the Second Ring Road, Andingmendong Dajie (✚ J2). Turn left into Guozijian Jie, a small street which heads west past the Temple of Confucius. Cycle down this street to the T-junction with Andingmennei Dajie. Turn left and at the traffic lights turn

Fine detail from the Lama Temple

right on to Guloudong Dajie (✚ H3), continuing to a junction by a large red building, Drum Tower. Turn left here on to Di'Anmenwai Dajie. A few hundred metres after a McDonald's restaurant turn right on to a lane, immediately after a humped bridge.

Follow the lane down to the lake and keep the water on your right as far as Di'Anmenxi Dajie (✚ G4). The rear entrance to Beihai Park is across the road. Turn left on to Di'Anmenxi Dajie and at the first junction with traffic lights turn right to rejoin Di'Anmenwai Dajie (the road with the humped bridge). Cycle south to the T-junction at the edge of Jingshan Park, turn left on to Jingshanhou Jie and follow the road around the park (there is an entrance on your right) to another T-junction (✚ G5). Go left on to Jingshanqian Jie and after passing the China Art Gallery turn right back on to Wangfujing. A picnic lunch from a supermarket, or takeaway, could be enjoyed in one of the parks.

THE SIGHTS

- Yonghegong (Lama Temple, ➤ 47)
- Temple of Confucius (➤ 46)
- Beihai Park (➤ 29)
- Jingshan Park (➤ 30)
- Forbidden City (➤ 31)
- China Art Gallery (➤ 54)

INFORMATION

Distance 10km
Time About 3 hours
Start/end point Wangfujing Dajie
✚ H5
🚌 104, 211

EVENING STROLLS

Street stalls selling western-style takeaway snacks are still uncommon

INFORMATION

Wangfujing
Distance 3km
Time About 1 hour excluding refreshment
Start point Beijing Hotel
H7
1, 4, 10, 37, 42, 57, 203
End point North of Forbidden City
G5
101, 103, 109, 111

Ritan Park
Distance 1.5km
Time 1 hour
Start/end point Jianguomen underground station
K6
Jianguomen

WANGFUJING

From the Beijing Hotel, turn left on to Wangfujing Dajie. The Beijing Department Store (► 76) and the Foreign Languages Bookstore (► 77) are both worth a browse. Try to reach the main junction with traffic lights around 6PM, where eating takes on a new dimension at the open-air food stalls down Dong'anmen Dajie, offering a healthy dose of culture shock. Further up Wangfujing, on the other side of the street, the Crowne Prince Hotel has a small art gallery off the foyer and further up, at No 26, the delightful Banpo Beer Hut (► 62) offers refreshment. At the top of Wangfujing turn left, and walk as far as the moat for a night view of the Forbidden City.

RITAN PARK

From Jianguomen underground station head east along Jianguomenwai Dajie and turn left at the International Club. The Russian Market (► 74) may still be open but the entrance to Ritan Park (► 52) is on the other side of the road. Go straight through the park as far as the circular walled area and then go right, keeping the playground on the left, before exiting on to Guanghua Lu and turning left. When you reach the British embassy, cross over and turn right into Xiushuidong Jie for a rear approach to the Silk Market (► 75). Alternatively, proceed as far as the traffic lights and turn right into Dongdaqiao Lu for drinks and food (► 68). Either journey will lead back on to Jianguomenwai Dajie for a stroll back to the station.

ORGANISED SIGHTSEEING

If your time is limited you can consider an organised tour, especially to sites outside the city like the Great Wall and the Ming Tombs (► 27, 28). Most hotels have a tour desk where you can make reservations. Prices vary so shop around.

EAS TRAVEL (CHINA CIVIL INTER-NATIONAL TOURIST CORPORATION)

Various tours and assistance with most aspects of a visit to the city, including accommodation in a good range of 2- and 3-star hotels.

✉ Bridge Mansion, 28 Dongsanhuanbei Lu, Chaoyang District ☎ 6594 6161; fax 6592 6717; e-mail eastvl@nihao.com. Web site at www.nihao.com/eastravel

Sample prices

The following prices are only a guide but a typical CITS city tour by bus like the one mentioned above is currently 340 yuan per person, including lunch, admission and tour guide. A morning-only city tour is 120 yuan and a trip to the Great Wall is 200 yuan. The *hutong* tour mentioned above is currently 180 yuan per person.

CITS (CHINA INTERNATIONAL TRAVEL SERVICE)

CITS desks can be found at the Jing Guang New World, Great Wall Sheraton, Kempinski and Hilton hotels. They conduct a variety of tours including a busy day tour by bus (Mon, Wed, Fri and Sat, 8:30AM) that visits the major sights: Tian'anmen Square, the Forbidden City, the Summer Palace and the Imperial Vault of Heaven.

In imperial times huge pots in the Forbidden City were filled with water in case of fire

Also available is a 7AM 'Morning Exercises with Local Chinese' tour. Being a big organisation, they tend to be more impersonal than those from EAS Travel.

✉ 28 Jianguomenwai Dajie, Chaoyang District ☎ 6515 8565; fax 6515 7798

BEIJING HUTONG TOURIST AGENCY

Tours of the *hutongs* (ancient city alleys or lanes) start at 8:50AM and 1:50PM from the agency's office found at the rear entrance of Beihai Park.

✉ 26 Di'anmenxi Dajie, Xicheng District ☎ 6615 9097/6400 2787

EXCURSIONS

Little bells tinkle to murmurs in the wind

FRAGRANT HILLS PARK

Popular with Beijingers as well as tourists, this accessible destination offers fresh air, bracing walks and superb views of the countryside from the top of the highest peak, reached by a chairlift or on foot. Once royal hunting territory, this was where Mao Zedong and his revolutionaries lived before moving to Beijing in 1949. Highlights include botanical gardens and the Temple of Brilliance (Zhao Miao), which, uniquely, escaped destruction by foreign troops in 1860 and 1900. Near the north gate entrance, the Indian-style Azure Clouds Temple (Biyun Si) is well worth visiting if only for the visual brilliance of its stupas (Buddhist tiered towers). Inside, there is a display relating to Sun Yat Sen (► 10) whose body was kept here for a while before being moved in the 1920s.

INFORMATION

Fragrant Hills Park
(Xiangshan Gongyuan)
Distance 20km west of Beijing
Journey time About 50 minutes

🚌 333 from the Summer
Palace; 360 from the zoo
(► 60); 318 from
Pingguoyuan

☎ 6259 1155
🕐 6AM—7PM
🎟 Cheap

Marco Polo Bridge (Lugouqiao)
Distance 16km south of Beijing
Journey time About 45 minutes
by bus

🚌 339
✉ Wanping City, Fengtai District
☎ 6381 5981
🕐 6AM—9PM
🎟 Cheap

MARCO POLO BRIDGE

The fact that Marco Polo never mentioned the Great Wall is one reason scholars question whether he ever made it to China. The Western name of this bridge derives from his putative 1290 visit and the detailed description of the bridge that he reported. Spanning the River Yongding, it was built in 1192, and restored in the 17th century, and is noted for an 18th-century stele with a calligraphic inscription by Emperor Qianlong. On each side of the bridge is a parapet with hundreds of carved lions surmounting the columns. In 1937 the bridge witnessed the opening shots in the war against the Japanese invasion. A museum near by is devoted to this event.

TIANJIN

There are two main attractions in China's fourth largest city and Beijing's nearest port: a wealth of colonial architecture, and superb antiques shopping. The old part of town, situated to the

Careful restoration has re-created these brilliant structures

INFORMATION

Tianjin

Distance 80km east of Beijing

Journey time 2 hours by bus or express train from Beijing

🚌 Buses depart from outside Beijing railway station

✉ There is no tourist office in Tianjin but the CITS office, 22 Yonyi Lu (opposite the Friendship Store), may be of some help.

☎ 022-8358 349/8358 501

❓ Organised trips from Beijing are available through CITS (► 19)

Peking Man

Distance 60km south-west of Beijing

Journey time About 2 hours by bus

🚌 From Haihutun bus station (get off in the village of Zhoukoudian), or by train from Yongdingmen railway station in Beijing

✉ Zhoukoudian, Fangshan District

☎ 6930 1272

🕐 8:30–4:30

💰 Cheap

south of the main railway station, has a number of old buildings dating back to the 19th century, when European imperial powers established themselves in the wake of a 'treaty' imposed by the British. The antiques market, based around Shenyang Jie, is especially worth a visit at weekends when the pavements are flooded with merchandise ranging from genuine antiques to inexpensive Mao memorabilia and related knick-knacks. Ideally one should come here on Saturday so as to catch the Sunday morning market around 9AM.

PEKING MAN SITE & MUSEUM

In 1921, excavations near the village of Zhoukoudian revealed evidence of palaeolithic Man – *Homo erectus Pekinensis* – dating back over 500,000 years. Bones of more than 40 individuals were identified. You can wander around the original site and, in an adjoining museum, see replicas of anthropological finds and remains of extinct creatures that must have terrified Peking Man. The original skull of Peking Man disappeared during World War II, when it was taken out of the country for safekeeping.

WHAT'S ON

JANUARY

Spring Festival Concert: in the Beijing Concert Hall (➤ 82). Classical Chinese music.

FEBRUARY

Chinese New Year: The most important festival in the Chinese calendar, falling in late January or early February, on the first day of the first moon. Celebrations are held in the Great Bell Temple (➤ 26), Ditan Park (➤ 52) and elsewhere. It is very much a family affair. Definitely a time to avoid travelling in China.
Lantern Festival: Also governed by the lunar cycle, it usually falls in February or March. One of the most colourful Chinese festivals; families celebrate in the evenings, especially in parks, with lanterns, carried by hand and placed on the ground around picnicking groups.

MARCH/APRIL

Guanyin's Birthday: A good time to visit temples. (Guanyin is the goddess of mercy.)

APRIL

Martial Arts Festival: Special martial displays take place, making this a good time to visit the Great Wall at Badaling (➤ 27).
Tomb Sweeping Day/Clear Brightness Festival (5 April most years, 4 April in leap years): Relatives pay their respects to their ancestors by sweeping and cleaning their tombs and burning ghost money.

MAY

May Day (1 May): International Labour Day is marked by splendid floral displays citywide and celebrations in Tian'anmen Square.
Youth Day: (4 May): Also marked by floral displays.

SEPTEMBER

China Arts Festival: organised by the Ministry of Culture (☎ 6403 1059). Details in the *China Daily*.
Mid-Autumn Festival: Marked by the giving of moon cakes, filled with a mixture of sweets and savouries – an acquired taste.

OCTOBER

National Day (1 October): The celebration of the founding of the People's Republic of China is marked by colourful flags, bunting, and red lanterns. Every five years an impressive military display takes place in Tian'anmen Square.

BEIJING's
top 25 sights

The sights are shown on the maps on the inside front cover and inside back cover, numbered **1–25** *from west to east across the city*

23

1

SUMMER PALACE (YIHEYUAN)

DID YOU KNOW?

- The Long Corridor, at 728m, is the longest painted corridor in the world
- Cixi kept her nephew, the emperor in name only, under house arrest for ten years in the Hall of Jade Ripples
- Emperor Qianlong sat on a nearby hill and watched 100,000 workers enlarging Kunming Lake
- The first automobile imported into China, a Mercedes-Benz, is still in the Summer Palace garage

A Summer Palace dragon

INFORMATION

➕ Off the map, 12km north-west of the city centre
✉ Yiheyuan, Haidian District
☎ 6288 1144
🕐 6:30–5
🍴 Coffee shop and restaurant
🚇 Xizhimen
🚌 301, 303, 332, 333, 346, 384, 904
💰 Moderate
↔ Old Summer Palace (➤ 25)

The playgrounds of modern millionaires seem very unimaginative in comparison with the pleasure grounds of the royal court. The largest imperial garden in China, it is strewn with palaces and architectural flights of fancy.

History Members of Beijing's imperial court needed a summer resort away from the Forbidden City and selected an area north-west of the city for this purpose. What you see today was laid out in the 18th century, but it was towards the end of the following century that Empress Dowager Cixi (➤ 12) misappropriated funds intended for the navy and spent it instead on a lavish rebuilding programme for her Summer Palace. Mindful, perhaps, of her debt to the navy, she commissioned the extraordinary Marble Boat that is berthed at the edge of the lake. The Summer Palace suffered in 1900 at the hands of Anglo-French troops intent on revenge after the Boxer Rebellion, but rebuilding began soon after. A major restoration was completed in the 1950s.

Walking guide After entering the grounds through the East Gate, note first the Hall of Benevolence and Longevity, where Cixi conducted official business with diplomats and courtiers. Stretched out behind the hall is the expanse of Kunming Lake. Keep it on your left, passing the Hall of Jade Ripples before entering the painted Long Corridor. Near the end of this walkway are a coffee shop, the ill-famed Marble Boat and a jetty where boat rides and rowing boats (or, in winter, skates) are available for trips to the 17-arched bridge which stretches from the shore to South Lake Island.

OLD SUMMER PALACE

The evocative 350-hectare grounds and ruins of the original Summer Palace quietly enchant today's visitors in a manner that will not endure if proposed schemes to turn the place into a theme park prove successful.

East meets West Remnants of baroque pillars and the ruins of grand fountains provide a tantalising hint of the artistic exuberance and sheer splendour that once characterised this royal playground. It was the creation of Emperor Qianlong in the second half of the 18th century and, though ostensibly created as an act of devotion to his mother, his project took on the feel of an audacious architectural binge. The emperor made half a dozen journeys south of the Yangtze river, accompanied by artists to make sketches, out of his desire to reproduce in the north the garden landscapes of southern China. He also commissioned European Jesuit architects, Sichelbarth and Benoist, to design Western buildings, including gazebos and follies, in an adventurous blending of West and East. The final result was three gardens: the Garden of Perfect Brightness, the Garden of Eternal Spring and the Garden of Beautiful Spring.

The Elgin masonry The broken masonry of the Old Summer Palace bears testimony to the destructive visit of British and French troops during the Second Opium War. In 1860, Lord Elgin ordered the site burned after his soldiers had thoroughly looted the place; some of their plunder may be seen in the British Museum and the Louvre. Today, there are ambitious, commercially motivated plans to restore the entire site; opposing the project are those who argue the ruins should stand as a historical record of past injustices.

HIGHLIGHTS

- Museum with models and drawings giving some idea of the pre-1860 splendour
- Restored concrete maze to the west of the fountain ruins
- Tranquil picnic places away from the metropolis

INFORMATION

- Off the map, about 2km east of the Summer Palace
- Qinghua Xilu, Haidian District
- 6255 1488
- 7–7
- Xizhimen
- 375 minibus from Xizhimen underground station
- Cheap
- Summer Palace (➤ 24)

Below: Part of the 10,000 Flowers Maze

GREAT BELL TEMPLE

Do not let the inconvenient location, or temple fatigue deter you from visiting this unique little museum. The experience is a rewarding one, and the music of the temple's Bell Orchestra is a surprising pleasure.

The technology The temple-museum is home to hundreds of bronze bells from all over China, but pride of place rests with a 46.5-tonne giant bell cast in the Ming dynasty known as the Yongle bell. It hangs on a huge wooden frame by a 1m-long iron and steel nail coated with copper. The nail is 6cm wide and pierces two U-shaped hooks around the wooden block. It is calculated that each square millimetre of the nail can withstand 2.4kg of shearing stress. Displays in the temple-museum (in English) explain the technology of bell-casting in China.

Ring the bells You can get into the spirit of bell-ringing by thumping a large one outside the temple with the help of a small battering ram. Inside the temple, for a nomi-

Fine design featuring bells, of course

nal fee, you can dip your hand into a large bowl of water before ferociously rubbing the twin handles to produce a musical vibration. If a certain frequency is attained the vibrations cause spurts of water to appear; hence the bowl is called the Dragon Fountain. A narrow staircase leads to a platform above the giant Yongle bell, where an interesting wall display is devoted to the bell's history. The music of the Great Bell Orchestra may be purchased in CD or cassette form. (If you buy one, check-play it on the temple's music system to make sure that your copy works.)

4

THE GREAT WALL

As President Nixon exclaimed to his Secretary of State, 'I think you would have to agree, Mr Secretary, that this is a great wall'. On some days the crowds of visitors also make it a great tourist circus.

Significance Mao Zedong said that anyone wishing to be a hero must first climb the wall, and for many Chinese people the wall remains very much a part of their cultural identity. It was built between the 5th century BC and the 16th century AD, its purpose was protective although it served also as a military communications route. From the 17th century onwards it was left to crumble away, helped by neighbouring peasants seeking building material.

Symbol of cruelty At odds with its contemporary significance, the building of the wall was often associated with acts of great cruelty. Emperors like Qin Shi Huang in the 3rd century BC became infamous for their mobilisation of enforced labour and there are stories of sections being made with the blood and bones of their builders.

Practicalities Ask a few questions before settling for one of the many available tours. Which part of the wall does the tour visit? Badaling, restored in the 1950s, is the most popular location but, be warned, the commercialism and crowds may disillusion you. A cable car helps the large number of visitors. Simatai requires a degree of fitness and fortitude, as sections of the unrestored wall are unprotected at the sides. Mutianyu is accessible and safe and, like Simatai, offers a cable-car ride up and down the side of the mountain. Where else does the tour go? Check how much time is spent at the wall, and beware of time-consuming and often unrewarding trips to factory shops along the way.

DID YOU KNOW?

- The wall is the only human-made structure discernible from the moon
- The wall's bricks could encircle the earth in a 5m-high wall
- Genghis Khan is said to have conquered the wall by simply bribing the sentries

INFORMATION

➕ Off the map to the north-west of the city

✉ Badaling in Yanqing County; Mutianyu in Huairou County; Simatai in Miyun County

☎ Badaling 6912 1235; Mutianyu 6964 2022; Simatai 6993 1095

🕐 Badaling Mon–Fri 6AM–6:30PM, Sat–Sun 6AM–10PM; Mutianyu 6:30AM–6PM; Simatai 8–5

🍴 Restaurants and teashops (£–££) at Badaling and Mutianyu

🚌 Tourist buses 1, 2, 3 from Qianmen terminus for Badaling; minibuses from Dongzhimen bus station for Mutianyu. No convenient access to Simatai by bus

🚇 Qinglongqiao

♿ None

💲 Moderate

↔ Ming Tombs (➤ 28) usually included in tours to Badaling or Mutianyu

❓ Hotels organise tours but prices vary; more expensive hotels tend to charge more

5

MING TOMBS

HIGHLIGHTS

- The mythological xiechi, a cat-like creature with horns, one of the six pairs of animals lining the Spirit Way
- The original, unpainted pillars supporting the Palace of Sacrificing, made from entire trunks of the nanmu tree
- Jewellery on show in the Palace of Sacrificing
- The royal treasures from Dingling found when the tomb was excavated

INFORMATION

- Off the map
- Shisanling, Changping County
- 6976 1424
- 7:30–6
- Most tours include lunch, at the Friendship Store (£–££)
- Tourist buses 1, 2, 3, 4, 5
- None
- Moderate
- Great Wall (➤ 27) usually included in tours to the Ming Tombs

Below: the main pavilion of the Ming Tombs

Willows whisper in the wind as the stone-carved figures along the Spirit Way stare imperiously at visitors following in the footsteps of the 17th-century mourners who carried the coffins of emperors to their final resting place.

Death of an emperor Of the 17 emperors who ruled during the Ming dynasty (1368–1644), 13 were ceremoniously laid to rest in this beautiful place about 30 miles north-west of their capital. The site was chosen for its geomantic qualities – facing Beijing, with mountains on three sides. Elaborate rites dictated the stages of the funeral; the deceased's concubines were also buried alive to comfort the emperor in the next world.

Not to miss The ceremonial avenue leading to the tombs, the Spirit Way, provides a wonderful opportunity to admire 18th-century Ming sculptures in their original context. Only three of the tombs are open to the public. At the end of the avenue one of them, Changling, comes into view. Emperor Yongle was interred here in 1424 and the focus of interest at this tomb is the imposing Palace of Sacrificing and its collection of imperial riches. A useful model of the whole site is on show and the exhibits carry descriptions in English. At the rear of the palace there is a stele tower, while an undistinguished mound behind railings at the back marks the actual burial ground. Of the other two tombs, only the excavated Dingling is worth a visit. A staircase leads to the burial vault holding a replica of the excavated coffin. In the courtyard, relics of the emperor and his two empresses are on display.

BEIHAI PARK

Kublai Khan is reputed to have created this, Beijing's largest imperial park. If you avoid weekends, Beihai Park – half water and half land – offers a placid charm and an opportunity to relax in the city.

History The lake in the park was dug during the Jin dynasty (12th–13th century), before the Forbidden City was thought of. All that remains of Kublai Khan's presence is a large, decorated jade vessel that was presented to him in 1265. It is now on show in the Round City, just inside the south entrance to the Park on Wenjin Jie. During the Qing dynasty Emperor Qianlong (1736–95) directed an ambitious landscaping project that laid the foundations for an exemplary Chinese classical garden. Jiang Qing, widow of Mao Zedong and a 20th-century empress of sorts, was a regular visitor during the 1980s.

What to see Inside the south gate is the Round City comprising a pavilion and courtyard. Beyond, the Hall of Receiving Light was originally a superior gatepost house for emperors and is now home to a Buddha crafted out of white jade, a present from Myanmar to Empress Dowager Cixi, who ruled from 1861 to 1908. From the hall the way leads to a short walk across the lake to Jade Island, noted for the White Dagoba, a 36m-high Buddhist shrine constructed in 1651 for a visit to Beijing by the Dalai Lama of Tibet. Also here is the famous Fangshan restaurant serving favourite imperial dishes, and a docking area where you can rent rowing boats. Off the island, the north shore has other places of interest (▶ Highlights panel).

HIGHLIGHTS

- The White Dagoba on Jade Island
- Elaborate, imperial-style Fangshan restaurant (▶ 62)
- Dragon Screen, on the north shore of the lake
- 17th-century Five Dragon Pavilions, near Dragon Screen
- Kublai Khan's jade vase, the largest of its kind in China
- Ice-skating or boating on the lake

INFORMATION

- ✚ F4/5, G4/5
- ✉ Wenjin Jie, Xicheng District
- ☎ 6404 0610
- 🕐 6AM–8PM
- 🍴 Snack and drink shops; Fangshan restaurant (▶ 62)
- 🚌 13, 101, 103, 107, 109, 111
- ♿ None
- 💰 Cheap
- ↔ Jingshan Park (▶ 30)

Detail from the Dragon Screen

JINGSHAN PARK

DID YOU KNOW?

- In 1644 the last Ming emperor is said to have hanged himself from a tree in the park. The spot is signposted and marked by a tree (not the original)
- Jingshan Park was not open to the public until 1928, and it was off limits again during the Cultural Revolution.

Reflection in a quiet corner of Jingshan Park

INFORMATION

- ✚ G5
- ✉ Jingshanqian Jie, Dongcheng District
- ☎ 6404 4071
- ⏰ 6AM–9PM
- 🚌 101, 103
- ♿ None
- 💰 Cheap

No other vantage point provides such a panoramic view of the Forbidden City's gold and russet roofscape as the top of the Pavilion of Everlasting Spring in Jingshan Park. Consider coming here before visiting the Forbidden City.

History As far back as the Yuan dynasty (1279–1368), Jingshan Park was the private recreational preserve for the imperial family. In the 15th century, when the moat for the Forbidden City was being dug, the demands of *feng shui* dovetailed with engineers' need to remove tons of earth. By using this to create large mounds north of the imperial palace, the royal residence was able to be put on high ground and thereby protected from malignant spirits. A story circulated that one emperor kept coal under one of the artificial hills; Coal Hill is another name for Jingshan Park.

Vantage point In addition to the compelling sight of the Forbidden City, the central pavilion – perched on the highest point in the park easily reached from the park's main entrance – also takes in views of the long lake in Beihai Park and its White Dagoba (▶ 29). On a clear day it is possible to see the Western Mountains to the north-west. The perspective of the city as a whole reveals how remarkably flat most of Beijing is, and it is easy to imagine the force of the biting winter winds scudding across the city.

Entertainment Back at the bottom you may catch a glimpse of a troupe of players dancing and cavorting as they lead a re-creation of an imperial procession, with the 'empress' in her sedan, to the sound of court music.

FORBIDDEN CITY (PALACE MUSEUM)

Wander off the beaten track here and imagine the past: emperors and empresses, concubines and eunuchs, court intrigues and decrees, palanquins, palaces and thrones. Make no mistake, this was the imperial heart of the Chinese civilisation.

Architecture No other complex in the world can match the Forbidden City in its harmonious mix of monumental scale, fine attention to detail, and geometry. The many individual buildings share a common style but the best achieve individuality by the generous use of open spaces. Begin a tour at the main entrance, the Meridian Gate (▶ 51), through the 10m wall that surrounds the complex with majestic watchtowers on its four corners. The wall itself is surrounded by a moat more than 50m wide.

All the main buildings in the Forbidden City are laid out on a north–south axis, starting from the south with the Halls of Supreme Harmony (Taihe) (▶ 36), Middle Harmony (Zhonge) (▶ 35) and Preserving Harmony (Baohe) (▶ 34). The Gate of Heavenly Purity (▶ 50) separates these official buildings from the residential quarter, the focal points of which are the Palace of Heavenly Purity (Qianqing Palace) (▶ 33) and the Palace of Earthly Tranquillity (▶ 33). Behind the royal bedrooms lies the Imperial Garden (▶ 32), which leads on to the northern exit.

Elitism Over 491 years (1420–1911), the residence and court of 24 emperors of the Ming and Qing dynasties imposed exclusivity to its limits here. Ordinary Chinese were barred from entering – hence the unofficial epithet. Most male employees were castrated; even so, many volunteered for the honour of working for the emperor.

DID YOU KNOW?

- The Forbidden City is the largest palace complex in the world
- There are 9,999 rooms (10,000 would have been hubris)
- Its construction required 100,000 craftsmen and one million labourers
- The Forbidden City was declared a World Heritage Site in 1987
- On average, more than 10,000 people a day come to see the complex
- Many of the finest treasures from here have been in Taiwan since 1949

INFORMATION

🕂 G5/6
✉ Xichang'an Jie, Dongcheng District
☎ 6513 2255
🕐 8:30–3:30
🍴 Snack shop (£) in the Imperial Garden
🚇 Qianmen
🚌 1, 4, 10, 22, 203
♿ None
💲 Moderate
↔ Many places of interest are in, or close to, the Forbidden City (▶ 30–6, 50–1)
❓ Taped guided tours in various languages can be rented at the southern entrance and returned at the northern exit.

9

IMPERIAL GARDEN (YU HUA GARDEN)

HIGHLIGHTS

- Rock garden
- Exhibition halls to the east of the garden
- Top of the north wall and view of Jingshan Park

INFORMATION

- ✚ G5
- ✉ Forbidden City
- ⏰ 8:30–3:30
- 🚇 Qianmen
- 🚌 1, 4, 10, 22, 203
- ♿ None
- 🎫 Included in admission fee to Forbidden City

A post-modern display in the highly classical Imperial Gardens

No run-of-the-mill tea and snack shop will be found in this classic traditional Chinese garden – instead, visitors enjoy refreshments in the 'Lodge for the Proper Places and Cultivation of Things'.

An imperial retreat There are four gardens within the Forbidden City but this one – some 90m by 130m – is the largest and most impressive. The arrangement of walkways, jade benches, pavilions and ponds was laid out during the Ming dynasty and, despite the fact that there are 20 buildings dotted around the place, the overall impression is of a relaxing natural setting. The imperial family had the Summer Palace (► 24) and other rural resorts to retreat to *en masse*, but the Imperial Garden (Yu Hua Yuan Garden), at the north end of the Forbidden City, was more readily available.

Repose The artificial rock garden arrangement, with a charming little temple perched on the summit, is one of the garden's most picturesque aspects. The large bronze elephants, with their faded gilt, contribute to an air of antiquity that is maintained by the centuries-old cypresses, which look as if they are close to the end of their natural lives. Surrounding bamboo plants are readily recognised but there are also other, rarer, plants in some of the flower beds.

Most visitors are justifiably weary by the time they reach the northern end of the Forbidden City so try to allow time to rest in the garden for a drink or a picnic if you can. An old lodge dispenses snacks, clean toilets are available, and there are some reasonably interesting tourist shops on the east side (► 72).

PALACE OF HEAVENLY PURITY

Doubtless many stories of passion and family intrigue unfolded here in the private bedrooms of the emperors and empresses. In 1542, Emperor Jiajing was nearly strangled in the Palace of Heavenly Purity (Qianqing Palace) by a maid.

Emperors at home Beyond the Gate of Heavenly Purity (► 50) lay the more private world of the Forbidden City, where the emperor lived with his family. The Palace of Heavenly Purity, during the Ming dynasty, was reserved as the bedroom of the emperor himself; the empress had her own quarters in the adjacent Palace of Earthly Tranquillity. The Qing dynasty preferred a less formal arrangement: royalty lived in other rooms to the east and west of the main buildings but the formal significance of the Palace of Heavenly Purity was not lost. When a Qing emperior died, his body was always placed in the Palace for a few days to signify he had lived a good life and had died while sleeping in his own bedroom. The successor to the throne was always announced from the Palace of Heavenly Purity.

Palace of Earthly Tranquillity This was the place for the consummation of royal marriages where the newly married emperor would spend the first days with his wife. The last emperor, Puyi, who came to the room in 1922 on his wedding night as a young teenager, reported as follows: 'The bride sat down on her bed, her head bent down. I looked around me and saw that everything was red: red bed-curtains, red pillows, a red dress, a red skirt, red flowers, and a red face... it all looked like a melted red wax candle. I did not know whether to stand or sit, decided I preferred the Hall of Mental Cultivation, and went back there.'

The imperial boudoir

HIGHLIGHTS

- Hall of Mental Cultivation (west of Palace of Heavenly Purity) (► 50)
- Exhibition halls and museums of imperial treasures (east of Palace of Earthly Tranquillity)

INFORMATION

- ✚ G5
- ✉ Forbidden City
- 🕐 8:30–3:30
- Ⓠ Qianmen
- 🚌 1, 4, 10, 22, 203
- ♿ None
- 🎫 Included in admission fee to Forbidden City
- ↔ Many nearby places of interest (► 30–6, 50–1)

11

HALL OF PRESERVING HARMONY

HIGHLIGHTS

- Dragon Pavement
- Marble Terrace
- Archaeological finds from the site, on display inside the hall
- Archery Pavilion (to the east of the hall)

INFORMATION

- G5
- Forbidden City
- 8:30–3:30
- Qianmen
- 1, 4, 10, 22, 203
- None
- Included in admission fee to Forbidden City

The solid marble Dragon Pavement

The marble Dragon Pavement at the rear of this hall, and the story of how it got here, is a graphic reminder of what the designers and builders of the Forbidden City achieved – and all without the aid of machinery.

Banquets and examinations The Hall of Preserving Harmony (Baohe Hall) is one of the Forbidden City's three great halls. Behind it, to the north, the Gate of Heavenly Purity (► 50) marks the division between the official, ceremonial sector to the south and the more private residential area to the north. At first, the Hall of Preserving Harmony was reserved for the royal banquets that usually concluded major ceremonial events. Later, during the rule of Emperor Yongzheng (1723–35) in the Qing dynasty, the notoriously difficult higher-level imperial examinations were held here. Successful candidates were assured of promotion to top-rank bureaucratic positions, so competition was intense.

Dragon Pavement Directly behind the hall, a broad marble walkway leads down from the terrace and forms the middle of a set of steps. It is known as the Dragon Pavement: a design motif depicts nine dragons flying above swirling clouds. Some 10,000 men were needed to excavate the marble; to transport the 250-tonne block the 50km from its quarry, wells were dug along the route to provide water, which was poured along the road and which formed a carpet of ice, since it was winter at the time. The marble block was pulled along this ice track, it is said, by up to 1,000 horses tied together.

HALL OF MIDDLE HARMONY

The Hall of Middle Harmony, or Zhonge Hall – a companion to the Hall of Supreme Harmony – is best viewed by standing on the marble terracing some distance away to appreciate how cannily the architects used open space to enhance the building.

Imperial dressing-room Of the three main halls aligned on the north–south axis of the Forbidden City, this is the smallest. It generally functioned as an all-purpose imperial hall. It was here that the emperor would be decked out in his fine regalia before proceeding due south to whatever important ceremony or event was taking place in the Hall of Supreme Harmony. Some relatively minor court procedures, such as the formal inspection of seeds before planting, would take place in the Hall of Middle Harmony. It was also where the emperor held audiences with high-ranking court officials or influential foreigners, and where dress rehearsals for various court rituals took place.

A smaller scale The Hall of Middle Harmony is not just a smaller version of the other two halls; it has its own unique features. First constructed in 1420, it was rebuilt in 1627 and the roof design, topped by a ball in its centre, is different but has the same overhanging eaves with decorative figures along the end of each ridge. The smaller size of this hall allows you to take in the harmonies of its proportions, without being overawed by the scale. The interior has a carpeted platform and a large, yellow, cushioned seat which was reserved for the emperor. The interior columns are not as richly embellished as those in the other two halls but the small squares that make up the ceiling are finely decorated.

DID YOU KNOW?

- The costume and regalia donned by the emperor varied for every event and were all laid down in regulations. Even the everyday gowns varied according to the day of the month: a black-and-white one inlaid with fur for the 19th day of the first lunar month and a sable one for the first day of the 11th month

INFORMATION

- G5
- Forbidden City
- 8:30–3:30
- Qianmen
- 1, 4, 10, 22, 203
- None
- Included in admission fee to Forbidden City
- Many nearby places of interest (➤ 30–6, 50–1)

13

HALL OF SUPREME HARMONY

HIGHLIGHTS

- The ornate coffered ceiling
- Richly decorated columns, carved with gold foil dragons
- The Dragon Throne and the nine-dragon screen behind it

INFORMATION

- ⊞ G6
- ✉ Forbidden City
- ◷ 8:30–3:30
- ⊕ Qianmen
- ▣ 1, 4, 10, 22, 203
- ▯ Included in admission fee to Forbidden City

The entire court population, many thousands in number, would wait in silence in the flagstoned area as the emperor ascended to his throne, then ritually kowtow nine times, as the eunuch choir rejoiced in song.

Supreme indeed Inside the Forbidden City, beyond the Meridian Gate (► 51), a courtyard leads to the Gate of Supreme Harmony and a stream crossed by five marble bridges. Two imposing bronze lions stand guard, the male holding an orb in his paw and the female a cub, a symbol of power and longevity. The vast courtyard ahead is dominated by the grandest single building in the Forbidden City, the Hall of Supreme Harmony or Taihe Hall. Here the robed emperor arrived in his yellow sedan chair to preside over important court ceremonies: coronations, royal birthdays, the winter solstice and the New Year. In the marble courtyard stood the armed, personal bodyguards, ceremonially dressed in red satin suits, while members of the royal family filled the marble staircase.

Symbolism The Hall of Supreme Harmony stands majestically upon a three-tiered terrace, with its own small courtyard surrounded by a marble balustrade. The stairway is furnished with bronze incense burners and in the courtyard are further symbols of longevity, bronze tortoises and cranes that have a space inside for burning incense. A pile of grains on the west side of the terrace and a sundial on the east symbolise the power of justice that resided with the imperial government. Entry to the hall is prohibited, but the splendid interior may be viewed from the open doorway.

Smoke wafted from the mouth of turtle-shaped incense burners

14

TIAN'ANMEN GATE

Imperial decrees were announced from the top of Tian'anmen Gate with dramatic aplomb – lowered in the beak of a gilded phoenix and received by the waiting dignitaries on their knees.

Historic entrance When China was under imperial rule, the gate formed the first entrance to the Forbidden City and served as the ritually ordained point for the emperor's edicts. As such, it seemed an appropriate platform for Chairman Mao Zedong's announcement, on 1 October 1949, to the waiting crowd and to the world at large, that 'the Chinese people have now stood up'. Here, too, in the 1960s, Mao broadcast to the million-strong ranks of Red Guards that the time for a 'cultural revolution' had arrived. A giant portrait of the Chairman hangs above the central portal (portraits of Mao are now rare in Beijing), with the slogan on its left reading 'Long Live the People's Republic of China', and on the right 'Long live the unity of the people of the world'. In 1989, student protesters raised a giant statue of a woman holding a torch of democracy, the Goddess of Liberty, to face Mao's portrait.

The seven bridges spanning the stream in front of the gate were not open to all and sundry; only the emperor could use the central bridge.

Iconography Tian'anmen Gate has become a highly charged icon, not only for Beijing but for China as a nation. At times, its image seems cheapened by being reproduced on everything from banknotes to tourist brochures. However, for the millions of Chinese who want to be photographed in front of it, the experience of being here is important, for its historical significance is deeply felt.

DID YOU KNOW?

- Chinese visitors like to rub the huge door knobs hoping that it will bring good luck
- For a less expensive rostrum view of Tian'anmen Square, use Zhengyangmen (Qianmen Gate ➤ 42)

PLA soldiers on duty at Tian'anmen Gate

INFORMATION

- ✚ G6
- ✉ Tian'anmen, Dongcheng District
- 🕐 8–5
- Ⓠ Qianmen
- 🚌 1, 4, 10, 22, 203
- 🎫 Moderate (free to pass through)

15

TIAN'ANMEN SQUARE

The most momentous events in modern Chinese history have taken place here. The square still resonates with memories of the masses gathered to witness the declaration of the People's Republic by Mao Zedong in 1949.

Communism's red star atop a clock tower

HIGHLIGHTS

- Chairman Mao Memorial Hall (south) (➤ 41)
- Great Hall of the People (west) (➤ 39)
- Museum of the Chinese Revolution (east) (➤ 43)
- Monument to the People's Heroes (centre) (➤ 40)

INFORMATION

- ✚ G7
- 🚇 Qianmen
- 🚌 1, 4, 10, 22, 203
- ♿ None
- 💲 Free
- ↔ Many places of interest are in, or close to, Tian'anmen Square (see 'Highlights' above and ➤ 42, 53,55)

A 20th-century gesture There had been a gathering place outside Tian'anmen Gate since the mid-17th century because squares are not part of the vocabulary of traditional Chinese town planning. Today's vast square, some 800m long by 500m wide, was not formally laid out until the 1950s, almost as a conscious political gesture towards a new vision of society. Packed crowds assembled here in 1949 to hear the declaration of the People's Republic. From 1966, vast rallies launched the Cultural Revolution from here, and in 1976 the deaths of Mao and Zhou Enlai brought millions of mourners to this spot. The importance of Tian'anmen Square for Chinese citizens is evidenced by its choice as a place of mourning and people's protest since the early 20th century. Mao Zedong's mausoleum (➤ 41) is here as well as the Monument to the People's Heroes (➤ 40) and, fittingly, the Great Hall of the People (➤ opposite).

Atmosphere Little prepares you for the experience of being in Tian'anmen Square. Its monumental dimensions can reduce everyone in it to disconcerting insignificance. Most Chinese visitors – tourists from every corner of the country – are as awestruck as foreigners by the colossal space and the cold, grey buildings on either side. The flying of a kite, music tinkling in the background and the taking of photographs add a much-needed human touch. Try to be here late one evening, when a gentler mood pervades the lonely space.

GREAT HALL OF THE PEOPLE

This huge building, where the National People's Congress meets when in session, was constructed in less than a year. The secret tunnels built for the safety of the People's Congress if meeting at the time of a world crisis, lead to the open space of Tian'anmen Square.

History The Great Hall of the People, occupying 200,000sq m, takes up the west side of Tian'anmen Square. Barring a session of the People's Congress – infrequently – the hall is open to the public. It was built in the late 1950s and the anonymous, monolithic architecture betrays its Stalinist origins. Margaret Thatcher tripped on the steps outside when visiting in 1982; in 1989 Gorbachev's entrance was blocked by ranks of demonstrators.

Sino-Soviet aesthetic The interior design is worth seeing as a definitive example of monumental scale seriously lacking in charm. The rooms are cavernous and forbiddingly grey in colour and mood. From the Central Hall, stairs lead upwards to the assembly hall and the guest hall, fronted by a huge landscape painting brought alive by an ideologically red sun. There are some 30 reception rooms, each named after a region or city (including Taiwan) and decorated in a style appropriate to that area. Some are open to public view. The Beijing Room is one of the most interesting, with three different-sized sets of chairs for the different ranks of those sitting on them. There is also an impressive mural of the Great Wall.

The way out of the Great Hall leads down to the basement, where there are uninspiring shops selling clothes and crafts.

DID YOU KNOW?

- The assembly hall, 75m wide and 60m long, has just under 10,000 seats and 500 recessed lights in its ceiling
- The banquet hall seats 5,000 guests at a time
- Rooms in the Great Hall are sometimes rented out to foreign companies for conventions

INFORMATION

- G7
- West side of Tian'anmen Square, Dongcheng District
- 6605 6847
- 8:30–3:30
- Qianmen
- 1, 17
- None
- Cheap

17

MONUMENT TO THE PEOPLE'S HEROES

DID YOU KNOW?

- The monument is made up of 17,000 pieces of granite and marble
- 10,000 workers, soldiers and peasants were said to have been consulted over the wording and appearance of the inscriptions

INFORMATION

- G7
- Tian'anmen Square, Dongcheng District
- Qianmen
- 1, 4, 10, 22, 203
- None
- Free

The monument is charged with past dramas

The central point in Tian'anmen Square is dedicated to all those who struggled for the glorious revolution. The monument site also carries a warning to the effect that anyone trying to start another one will be sternly punished.

Heroes of the nation The foundations of the 38m-high granite and marble obelisk were laid on the eve of 1 October 1949 – the day that the establishment of the People's Republic was announced – but the monument was not officially unveiled to the public until 1958. The inscription on the north-facing side carries words of praise by Mao for all those who died struggling for the country's independence, 'Eternal glory to the nation's heroes'. A similar inscription on the south-facing wall carries the words of Zhou Enlai. The base of the monument is decorated with a series of bas-reliefs showing key scenes from China's revolutionary history. A graphic scene, on the east-facing side, shows Chinese people burning the opium that the British introduced into China in the 19th century.

No wreaths, please The two-tier platform upon which the obelisk stands is now closed off to the public and kept under guard; a sign indicates that any laying of wreaths or commemorative gestures is strictly outlawed. In 1976, after the death of the immensely popular Zhou Enlai, anti-government riots broke out when wreaths laid at the monument were removed. Again, in 1989, the wreaths laid to commemorate the death of a politician who had been dismissed by the government became the catalyst for student demonstrations. On 13 May of that year some 200 students pedalled to the square and launched a hunger strike around the monument.

CHAIRMAN MAO MEMORIAL HALL

Copies of the **Little Red Book** *and other Mao memorabilia may be cynically peddled to tourists, but millions of ordinary Chinese still have a deep respect for Mao Zedong. A visit to his mausoleum makes this very obvious.*

Exterior The Memorial Hall, behind the Monument to the People's Heroes at the south end of Tian'anmen Square, was completed in 1977 by volunteer labour, only one year after the death of the famous helmsman of the Chinese people. To date, it has seen some 110 million visitors. The inscription above the entrance, 'Chairman Mao Mausoleum', was calligraphed by Hua Guofeng who succeeded Mao to the leadership of the Communist Party. The two-tiered structure is supported by 44 octagonal granite columns.

Interior Visitors enter the hallowed ground through a vast anteroom dominated by a large white statue of Mao. The line of visitors moves forward inexorably into the main memorial hall where the embalmed body lies in a crystal coffin in a gloomy orange light, draped with the red flag of the Chinese Communist Party. It only takes a couple of minutes to file past the coffin. Photography is strictly forbidden. The mood is sombre and reverent.

Technology The body is raised from its freezer each morning and descends after the last of the morning pilgrims. A number of apocryphal stories are told regarding the problems of maintaining the body and these gained credence when, in 1998, the mausoleum reopened after a nine-month 'renovation' – looking the same as it ever did.

DID YOU KNOW?

- No other Chinese leader's body has been preserved
- The government overruled Mao's wish to be cremated
- 22 litres of formaldehyde went into Mao's corpse
- A dissident who publicly called for Mao's cremation in 1997 was exiled

INFORMATION

- ✚ G7
- ✉ South end of Tian'anmen Square, Dongcheng District
- ☎ 6513 2277
- 🕐 8–11:30 and 2–4 (closed PM on Tue, Thu and Sat)
- 🚇 Qianmen
- 🚌 1, 4, 10, 22, 203
- 🎫 Free

An inspiring statue outside the mausoleum

QIANMEN GATE (ZHENGYANGMEN)

HIGHLIGHTS

The view from the top of the gate takes in:

- Chairman Mao Memorial Hall (immediately to the south) (➤ 41)
- Tian'anmen Square (to the south) (➤ 38)
- Great Hall of the People (west) (➤ 39)
- Museum of the Chinese Revolution (east) (➤ 43)

INFORMATION

- ✚ G7
- ✉ Tian'anmen Square, Dongcheng District
- ◷ 8:30–4
- 🚇 Qianmen
- 🚌 1, 17
- ♿ None
- 💷 Cheap

The entrance to the Gate is less forbidding than in imperial times

The emperors took their security seriously: a moat and wall ringed their private city and another large wall surrounded the inner city. All that remains of this is the large central portal of Zhengyangmen (or Qianmen Gate); giving a sense of the monumental scale of Tian'anmen Square .

History Entry into the Forbidden City was simply not an option for the general public; even access to the inner city was controlled by a series of nine guarded gates. On the south side of Beijing, Zhengyangmen was the main point of transit between the inner city and the residential areas outside.

The gate was constructed during the rule of Emperor Yongle in the first half of the 15th century. A sister gate (Jianlou), is clearly visible across the road to the south but, unlike Zhengyangmen, it is not open to the public. Originally, these two gates were joined by walls.

Visiting the gate When you stand with the Chairman Mao Memorial Hall behind you, the ticket booth is on the corner of the left side of the gate, while the entrance itself is on the east side. Inside, there are three levels. The first is a gallery of black-and-white photographs relating to Chinese history, with brief explanations in English. The second is filled with fairly uninspiring souvenir shops, and the third level has a more interesting shop devoted to tea-drinking.

Outdoors are stone tables that may be used for snacks or picnics; Western take-away food is available across the road opposite Qianmen underground station.

MUSEUM OF THE CHINESE REVOLUTION

Anyone unfamiliar with modern Chinese history should find half a day to spend at this excellent museum representing the history of injustice and suffering in graphic detail. Highly recommended.

History Architecturally a sister building to the Great Hall of the People, the Museum of the Chinese Revolution looms over the east side of Tian'anmen Square. The interior is far more fascinating than the exterior suggests; note that its easy to confuse the museum's ticket booth and entrance with that of the Museum of Chinese History (▶ 55) which occupies the southern half of the same building, so be alert on the way in so that you don't end up in the wrong place. After 1966, during the tumultuous Cultural Revolution, the museum was closed down but it is not clear why, as the contents conclude with the founding of the Republic in 1949. Until 1 July 1997, a giant digital clock outside the museum counted down the days, hours and seconds to the return of Hong Kong.

Interior The Modern China Exhibition (1840–1949) on the ground floor is the focus for any visit. English translations with the exhibits provide a crash course in modern Chinese history. A lot of the material on display is based around documents and enlarged photographs, which are usually well chosen and superbly rendered. Exhibitions cover the Opium Wars, the 1911 revolution, the foundation of the Communist Party in 1921, the Japanese invasion of 1937 and the war of resistance – all leading up to Mao Zedong's momentous declaration of independence.

HIGHLIGHTS

- Photographs relating to the Opium Wars
- Exhibition room devoted to the Japanese invasion
- View from the window across Tian'anmen Square

INFORMATION

- ✚ H7
- ✉ East side of Tian'anmen Square, Dongcheng District
- ☎ 6526 3355
- 🕐 8:30–5 (last entry 4:15)
- 🚇 Qianmen
- 🚌 1, 4, 17, 57
- 💰 Cheap

A stimulating introduction to modern Chinese history

21

QINIAN HALL

Through the perfection and harmony of its proportions, this triple-roofed temple – the Hall of Prayer for Good Harvests – achieves a state of both ultra-modernism and sacred serenity. It represents the highest development of religious architecture in China and should not be missed.

The finest temple in Beijing

DID YOU KNOW?

- The trees used for the Dragon Fountain pillars were imported from Oregon
- The roof was built without nails or cement
- The number of tiles used exceeds 50,000

INFORMATION

- ✚ H9
- ✉ Tiantandong Lu, Chongwen District
- ☎ 6702 2617
- ◷ 6AM–8PM
- 🚍 6, 15, 17, 20, 35, 39, 43, 106
- ♿ Cobbled ramp at the west entrance to ground level
- 🍴 Cheap
- ↔ Imperial Vault of Heaven (➤ 45), Beijing Natural History Museum (➤ 54)
- ❓ Audio-taped tours available

Tiantan Qinian Hall, or Hall of Prayer for Good Harvests is part of Tiantan, the Temple of Heaven, the largest group of temple buildings in China. Tiantan Park surrounds the temple off the north–south axis that aligns the major buildings in the Forbidden City. Ming and Qing emperors ceremoniously travelled the short journey south to Tiantan to offer sacrifices to heaven in springtime and at the winter solstice. Before the first Ming emperor made this sacred journey in the 15th century this area was associated with religious rituals as far back as the Zhou dynasty (11th century BC–256 BC).

Qinian Hall First built in 1420 and completely restored in 1889 after a lightning strike, the hall was where the emperor prayed for a good harvest. It is an extraordinary structure: three storeys and a three-tiered roof, with blue-glazed tiles, rising above marble terraces and seeming to float in the air.

The four central columns, the Dragon Fountain pillars, represent the four seasons, and the outer rings, of 12 columns each, represent the months of the year and the twelve divisions of the day or 'watches'. The complex artwork of the caisson ceiling, with a wood-sculptured dragon in the centre, is best appreciated with binoculars. In the courtyard, south of the hall, one of the buildings has been converted into a large arts and crafts shop.

IMPERIAL VAULT OF HEAVEN

Here, Ming emperors dressed in sacrificial robes, consulted their ancestors' tablets before ceremoniously ascending the steps of the Circular Mound Altar and performing rituals that had been refined over the centuries.

Interior design is the highlight of the Imperial Vault of Heaven

Wooden temple From the Gate of Prayer for Good Harvests, a raised walkway leads to the Imperial Vault of Heaven. Built entirely of wood, it is an octagonal vault with a double-eaved roof; originally built in 1530, it was rebuilt in the mid-17th century. In many respects it is a smaller version of the Qinian Hall, with a similar blue-tiled roof, to represent heaven, but it receives more light and so it's easier to appreciate the elegant artwork inside.

Echoes and more echoes Surrounding the Imperial Vault of Heaven is the Echo Wall, so-called because of its acoustic property, which allows two people standing alongside the wall to converse at a distance. Additionally, in the courtyard, at the foot of the staircase, the first stone is said to generate one echo, the second stone two echoes, while a single clap or shout from the third stone produces three echoes.

Circular Mound Altar (Round Altar) This huge round altar, south of the Imperial Vault of Heaven, is not as impressive as the other buildings of Tiantan, but its symbolism is highly charged and it is in fact the Altar of Heaven itself. The three marble tiers of the altar symbolise earth, man, and heaven and, according to Chinese cosmology, the central stone in the top tier marks the very centre of the world. On the winter solstice, the emperor ascended to this spot and from a stone tablet read sacred prayers of indulgence.

HIGHLIGHTS

- Bridge of Vermilion Stairs leading to the Imperial Vault
- Coffered ceiling of the Imperial Vault, displaying a gilded dragon playing with a pearl
- Echo Wall and Echo Stones
- View of the Imperial Vault from the top tier of the Circular Mound Altar (Round Altar)

INFORMATION

- ✚ H10
- ✉ Tiantandong Lu, Chongwen District
- ☎ 6702 2617
- 🕐 6AM–8PM
- 🚍 6, 15, 17, 20, 35, 39, 43, 106
- ♿ None
- 🎫 Entrance charge included in ticket for Qinian Hall
- ↔ Qinian Hall (► 44), Beijing Natural History Museum (► 54)
- ❓ Audio-taped tours available

45

23

TEMPLE OF CONFUCIUS

HIGHLIGHTS

- 700-year-old cypress tree
- Hall of Great Achievements
- Steles in the courtyard

INFORMATION

- ✚ J2
- ✉ Guozijian Jie, Dongcheng District
- ☎ 6407 3593
- 🕐 8:30–5
- 🚌 13, 113, 104, 108
- ♿ None
- 💰 Cheap
- ↔ Yonghegong (Lama Temple) (➤ 47)

Examination successes were recorded for posterity

Situated down an ancient hutong, *with commemorative arches over the doorways, the Temple of Confucius is a quiet refuge from the tourist track.*

Confucius This noted philosopher and teacher (551–479 BC) taught the virtues of moderation, family piety and nobility of mind through good behaviour. His conservative belief in the natural hierarchy of the ruler and subject won his ideology the favour of the emperors and, despite fierce criticism from the Communist Party, the influence of Confucius is still felt in Chinese society today.

Outside the temple Occupying the forecourt area are a number of cypress trees including an ancient one that is supposed to have been planted when the temple was built in the fourteenth century. The other notable feature is a collection of some 190 steles that record the names of candidates who, between 1416 and 1904, successfully passed the notoriously severe civil service examinations. Adjoining the temple stands the Imperial College, now called the Capital Library, where the emperor would deliver his annual lecture on classic Confucian texts. Stone tablets recording the texts are in a nearby courtyard of their own.

The interior The Temple of Confucius, built in 1302 and restored in 1411, does not contain any statues of the philosopher himself, but in the Hall of Great Achievements, the central altar contains a small wooden tablet dedicated to his memory. Emperors and high ranking scholars came here to make offerings to the spirit of Confucius and conduct ancient rituals. Part of the temple is now the Capital Museum, housing an array of ritual implements used in the temple.

LAMA TEMPLE (YONGHEGONG)

Undoubtedly the liveliest functioning temple in Beijing, colourful and exciting, redolent of incense, and as popular with worshippers as with tourists.

From palace to lamasery Built in 1694, this was the residence of Yongzheng, a son of Emperor Kangxi, until, in 1723, the son became the new emperor. Following imperial tradition, his former house was converted to a temple and in 1744 it became a lamasery – a monastery for Tibetan and Mongolian Buddhist monks. Closed down during the Cultural Revolution, but saved from destruction by deputy prime minister Zhou Enlai, the Lama Temple reopened in 1980 as a functioning monastery with monks from Mongolia. It has been suggested that the place is a showcase exercise in public relations, designed to demonstrate how the Chinese state tolerates Tibetan Buddhism. However, it has lovely gardens and a wonderful interior.

Layout The temple is a complex of halls and courtyards with a variety of interesting pavilions on either side. In the first hall, the Hall of Celestial Kings, giant guardians flank a lovely smiling, rotund buddha. The next hall, the Hall of Eternal Harmony, has three buddhas accompanied by 18 disciples. Beyond the next courtyard lie the Hall of Eternal Protection and the Hall of the Wheel of Law (the law being the cycle of death and rebirth). The final hall, the Wanfu Pavilion, contains a 23m-high buddha, carved in the mid-18th century from a single sandalwood tree transported from Tibet, and also flanked by guardians. A wonderful figure of a god with at least 30 hands is the focus of the Esoteric Hall, on the temple's east side. One of two halls with the same name, it was used as a place of scholarship for the study of scriptures.

Lama Temple's characteristic flamboyant eaves

HIGHLIGHTS

- Maitreya Buddha in the Wanfu Pavilion
- Hall of Eternal Harmony (Yonghedian)
- Prayer wheel in the Pavilion of Perpetual Peace (west of Wanfu)

INFORMATION

- ✚ J2
- ✉ Yonghegong Dajie, Beixinqiao, Dongcheng District
- ☎ 6404 3769
- 🕐 9–4
- 🚇 Yonghegong
- 🚌 13, 62, 116
- 🎫 Cheap
- ↔ Temple of Confucius (➤ 46)

25

ANCIENT OBSERVATORY

Explore centuries of Chinese astronomy through the range of star-gazing paraphernalia on display in a corner tower of the city's walls. City views from the roof will please even the museum-shy visitor.

HIGHLIGHTS

- 4500-year-old pottery jar with pictographic solar patterns
- Star map from Song dynasty (13th century)
- Equatorial armilla of 1673
- Views of the city from the roof of the tower

INFORMATION

- ✚ K7
- ✉ 2 Dongbiaobei Hutong, Jianguomennei Dajie
- ☎ 6524 2202
- ◐ 9–11 and 1–4 (closed Mon and Tue)
- ◉ Jianguomen
- ▤ 1, 4, 9, 10, 43, 103, 403
- ♿ None
- ▥ Cheap

These original instruments were first installed by Jesuit missionaries

West meets East In the 13th century Kublai Khan founded an observatory near the present site, building on a Chinese tradition that was already well established. Islamic scientists were in charge in the early 17th century and when Jesuit missionaries arrived in Beijing, they astonished the court by their ability to make astronomical forecasts and soon found themselves in charge of the observatory. New instruments were installed, and the Jesuits remained until the early 19th century. In 1900, French and German troops stole many of the instruments; they were later returned.

What to see At ground level, on the other side of the entrance booth, a small open-air area displays reproductions of astronomical instruments. Also on ground level is a small museum with explanations (in English) of the main exhibits. These include a copy of the world's oldest astronomical account, a 14th-century record of a supernova. Steps lead up to the top of the tower, and on the roof there are eight original instruments – including a sextant, a theodolite, a quadrant and an altazimuth – most were made in the 17th century. Back at ground level, the small rear garden contains more reproductions of celestial instruments as well as stone carvings recording constellations and solar eclipses. An interesting little shop there sells small replicas of astronomical instruments, and just outside the main entrance is a jewellery shop (▶ 72).

BEIJING's
best

GATES & HALLS

See Top 25 sights for
HALL OF PRESERVING HARMONY
(BAOHE HALL) (► 34)

Concubines and eunuchs

The majority of the thousands of inhabitants of the inner court of the Forbidden City were either concubines or eunuchs; most were recruited from the poor, and although a few became important and influential figures, the majority were little better than slaves. However, young men volunteered to become eunuchs because it was seen as an honour and at the height of the Ming dynasty there were some 25,000 court eunuchs.

A symbol of well-being and an assured future in China

ESOTERIC HALL

Of the two halls of this name in the Lama Temple, the more interesting is on the right (east) side as you walk through the temple from the entrance. It was a place of scholarship for the study of scriptures, its focus of interest today is a wonderful figure of a god with a least 30 hands.

➕ J2 ✉ Yonghegong Dajie, Beixinqiao, Dongcheng District ☎ 6404 3769 🕐 8:30–4 🚇 Yonghegong 💰 Cheap

GATE OF HEAVENLY PURITY

The Gate of Heavenly Purity divides the official ceremonial buildings of the Forbidden City from the private inner court of residential rooms. During the Qing dynasty, state officials were sometimes granted an audience here with the emperor. Two gilded bronze lions sit before the gate, the female clutching an upturned cub, symbol of prosperity, in her paw while the male grips an orb, symbol of authority, in his claw.

➕ G5 ✉ Xichang'an Jie, Dongcheng District ☎ 6513 2255 🕐 8:30–5 🍴 Snack shop (£) in the Imperial Garden 🚇 Qianmen 💰 Moderate (included in entrance ticket to Forbidden City)

HALL OF MENTAL CULTIVATION (YANGXINDIANG)

One of the many private rooms on the west side of the northern half of the Forbidden City, this hall was home to Empress Dowager Cixi (► 12). It also used by the last emperor, Puyi, as a private bedroom.

➕ G5 ✉ Xichang'an Jie, Dongcheng District ☎ 6513 2255 🕐 8:30–5 🍴 Snack shop (£) in the Imperial Garden 🚇 Qianmen 💰 Moderate (included in entrance ticket to Forbidden City)

HALL OF UNION

Hall of Union standing between the Palace of Heavenly Purity (► 33) and the Palace of Earthly Tranquillity, is the middle of the three inner halls in the northern, residential area of the Forbidden City. During the Qing dynasty it was used for royal birthdays and coronations. It now contains a set of imperial jade seals, a glockenspiel and an 18th-century clepsydra, a time-measuring device worked by the flow of water.

🛇 G5 ⊠ Xichang'an Jie, Dongcheng District ☎ 6513 2255 🕘 8:30–5 🍴 Snack shop (£) in the Imperial Garden 🚇 Qianmen ♿ None 💷 Moderate (included in entrance ticket to Forbidden City)

MERIDIAN GATE (WUMEN)

This is the largest and most important of the four entrance gates to the Forbidden City. Only the emperor could normally use the central one of its five arched portals, but exceptions were made for the empress on her wedding day and also for the three candidates who gained the highest marks in each year's imperial examinations, who were allowed to use the gate once. From the Meridian Gate the emperor would inspect his army, pass sentence on the captured troops of defeated armies, and present the New Year's calendar to his court officials. The present U-shaped, multi-eaved gate dates back to the 17th century when it was substantially restored.

🛇 G6 ⊠ Xichang'an Jie, Dongcheng District ☎ 6513 2255 🕘 8:30–5 🍴 Snack shop (£) in the Imperial Garden 🚇 Qianmen ♿ None 💷 Moderate (included in entrance ticket to Forbidden City)

SHENWU GATE

Shenwu (Gate of Spiritual Prowess) is the northern gate of the Forbidden City, built in 1420. Each morning, to announce the dawn, the bell was rung 108 times, followed by the drum. The procedure was repeated at dusk. Every three years, the girls selected as concubines used Shenwu to enter the palace. The tower, which gives good views across to Jingshan Park, can be reached by the a long ramp. It contains an exhibition related to the architecture of the Forbidden City (explanations in Chinese only).

🛇 G5 ⊠ Jingshanqian Jie, Dongcheng District ☎ 6513 2255 🕘 8:30–5 🍴 Snack shop (£) in the Imperial Garden 🚇 Qianmen ♿ None 💷 Moderate (included in entrance ticket to Forbidden City)

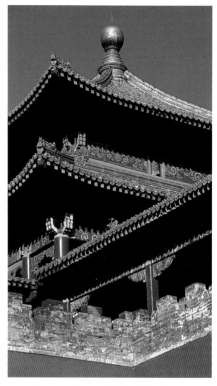

One of the five towers adding majesty to the Meridian Gate

Feng shui

Literally 'wind and water', *feng shui* is the ancient Chinese system of geomancy that is used to determine the most propitious design and position for buildings. Today, *feng shui* experts are often consulted before the plans for a new building are finalised. They employ the same principles as those that governed the layout of the Forbidden City.

51

PARKS

An unusual pictorial display in the heart of Ritan Park

Tai chi

This form of spiritual exercise, sometimes known as 'shadow boxing', is best appreciated when observed *en masse* in Beijing's public parks from around 6 to 8AM. It is particularly popular with older citizens and consists of slow, balletic movements of the limbs designed to balance the flow of energy (chi) through the body and attain a healthy spiritual poise.

See Top 25 Sights for
BEIHAI PARK (► 29)
JINGSHAN PARK (► 30)
OLD SUMMER PALACE (► 25)
SUMMER PALACE (► 24)
TIANTAN PARK(► 44, 45)

DITAN PARK

Conveniently close to an underground station and the colourful Yonghegong (Lama Temple ► 47), Ditan (Temple of Earth) Park dates to the early 16th century when it was built for emperors to offer sacrifices to heaven. The original altar is now part of a small museum (£) which also displays an imperial sedan.
➕ J1/2 ✉ Andingmenwai Dajie, Dongcheng District ☎ 6421 4657
🕐 6AM–9PM Ⓜ Yonghegong ♿ None 💷 Cheap

GRAND VIEW GARDENS (DAGUANYUAN PARK)

Laid out in the 1980s as part of a project to film the 18th-century classic Chinese novel *The Dream of the Red Mansion*, this is a pleasant place, away from the city centre, with a strange artificial rock formation, a water pavilion and walkways around a lake. Readers of the novel may recognise some literary locations.
➕ C10 ✉ Nancaiyuan Jie, Xuanwu District ☎ 6351 8879
🕐 8:30–5:30 🚌 19, 59 ♿ None 💷 Cheap

RITAN PARK

Ritan (Temple of the Sun) Park developed out of a 16th-century altar site where the emperor made sacrificial offerings to the sun god. Situated in the heart of embassy-land, near the Friendship Store (► 72, 74) and the Russian market (► 74), it makes for a pleasant evening stroll (► 18).
➕ L6 ✉ Ritan Lu, Chaoyang District ☎ 6502 1743
🕐 6:30AM–8:30PM 🍴 Restaurant in north-east corner of park
🚌 1, 4, 9, 29, 48, 57, 103 ♿ Few 💷 Cheap

TAORANTING PARK

The first park here was laid out in the Liao period (947–1125) and during the Qing dynasty it became one of the few parks open to the public. Its swimming pool is a big draw with Chinese families but there are quiet places to retreat to, including the remains of a monastery and a number of pavilions (this is also known as Joyous Pavilion Park).

✚ F10 ✉ Taiping Jie, Xuanwu District 🕐 6AM–10PM 🚌 14 from Hepingmen underground station ♿ None 💰 Cheap

TUANJIEHU PARK

This delightful little park, surrounded by high-rise office blocks, off the tourist trail, offers a relaxing diversion from palaces and shops. Paths lead through a scenic arrangement of lake, willow trees, humped bridge and greenery. There is a small amusement park with bumper cars for toddlers.

✚ N5 ✉ Dongsanhuanbei Lu, Chaoyang District ☎ 6507 3603 🕐 6:30AM–9PM 🍴 Asian Star restaurant (➤ 66) 🚌 43, 115 ♿ Few 💰 Cheap

ZHONGSHAN PARK

This park, south-west of the Forbidden City, opened to the public in 1924 and, later dedicated to Sun Yat Sen, leader of the 1911 revolution and the country's first president. In imperial times it was the site of an altar, built in 1421 but still standing, where the emperor made twice-yearly sacrifices. Now, ancient cypresses shade locals and tourists alike and there is a children's play area.

✚ G6 ✉ 64 Xichang'an Jie, west of Tian'anmen Square, Dongcheng District ☎ 6605 5431 🕐 6:30AM–7PM 🚇 Qianmen ♿ None 💰 Cheap

ZIZHUYUAN PARK

Especially appealing, 'Purple Bamboo Park' is famous for its abundant bamboo,(whether there is any hint of purple in its colour is debatable). One third of the 47 hectares consists of lakes and rivers, and a variety of trees and shrubs ensure delightful arboreal views.

✚ A2/3 ✉ Baishiqiao Lu, Haidian District ☎ 6842 0055 🕐 6AM–8PM 🍴 Restaurants (££) at New Century Hotel (➤ 84) 🚇 Xizhimen ♿ Few 💰 Cheap

Youngsters enjoying a snack outdoors

Park life

In recent years, Western-style disco-dancing has become popular with middle-aged citizens as a form of exercise. Early in the morning they arrive with cassette players and even the occasional boom box, while alongside them more sedate movements are played out by tai chi devotees. Elderly men like to stroll with their bird-cages or sit and listen to the warbling of caged finches and orioles; nearby, affectionate young couples enjoy the relative privacy of parks to smooch on benches.

53

MUSEUMS AND GALLERIES

See Top 25 Sights for
FORBIDDEN CITY (▶ 31–6)
MING TOMBS (▶ 28)
MUSEUM OF THE CHINESE REVOLUTION (▶ 43)

Lu Xun

Hailed as the most progressive modern Chinese writer, Lu Xun (1881–1936), gave up a career in medicine to become a satirical writer. His most famous work, a short story, *The True Story of Ah Q,* is well worth reading. Copies in translation may be purchased at the Lu Xun Museum.

A bust of Lu Xun

Exhibits at the Natural History Museum

BEIJING ART MUSEUM OF STONE CARVINGS

On the site of the Wuta (Five-Pagoda) Temple (▶ 57), the museum contains 600 stone carvings from the Han, the late Qing dynasty. The explanatory text is not translated but sometimes an English-speaking guide is available. Rubbings of the stone-carved steles can be made. There is a collection of tombstones, some with Latin inscriptions recording the deaths of 17th-century Jesuit missionaries.

🔢 B2 ✉ 24 Wutasi, Baishiqiao, Haidian District ☎ 6217 2894/ 6218 6081 🕒 8:30–4 🍴 Nearby restaurant (▶ 62) 🚇 Xizhimen 🚹 None 💰 Cheap

BEIJING NATURAL HISTORY MUSEUM

This place is rather unique and strange. The ground floor is devoted to zoology and is by turns dull and kitschy, but upstairs, under the guise of anthropological study, a horror show displays cross-sections of human cadavers and pickled organs. Come back another time if a school trip is in evidence.

🔢 G9 ✉ 126 Tianqiaonan Dajie, Chongwen District ☎ 6702 4431 🕒 8:30–5 (last ticket 4) 🍴 American-style fast-food outlet next door (£) 🚌 2, 25, 53, 59, 120, 803 🚹 None 💰 Cheap

CHINA ART GALLERY

Situated in one of the first big buildings to appear after 1949, this is the city's major art gallery and China's national art museum. Visiting international exhibitions (details in the *China Daily*) are held on the ground floor. Contemporary Chinese art is displayed upstairs. No socialist realism here: the subject matter is Chinese life, especially scenes of rural activity, and the

style is pictorial and mostly Western.
➕ H5 ✉ 1 Wusi Dajie, Dongcheng District ☎ 6401 2252
🕐 Tue–Sun 9–4 🚍 103, 104, 109, 111, 112 ♿ None 💷 Cheap

FORMER RESIDENCE OF SOONG QING-LING

Soong Qing-Ling, the wife of Sun Yat Sen, lived in this former Qing mansion – home to the father of China's last emperor – from 1963 until her death in 1981. Quite apart from the exhibits relating to her life, the gardens are exquisite and worth a visit.
➕ F2 ✉ 46 Houhaibeiyan, Xicheng District ☎ 6403 5858/ 6404 4205 🕐 9–4 🚍 5, 55 ♿ None 💷 Cheap

LU XUN MUSEUM

Situated next to the compound where the writer Lu Xun (► panel opposite) lived for a short time, the museum contains drawings with revolutionary themes, and material relating to his life and times, including the furniture of his study and bedroom. There are no explanations in English.
➕ D4 ✉ 19 Gongmenkou 3 Tiao, Xicheng District ☎ 6616 4169 🕐 Tue–Sun 9–4 🚇 Fuchengmen ♿ None 💷 Cheap

MILITARY MUSEUM

Dedicated to the history of the People's Liberation Army (PLA), this museum's graphic displays engage most visitors. The examples of Socialist Realist paintings and early photographs of Mao Zedong are especially interesting. Larger artefacts include a frigate armed with missiles and US tanks captured in the Korean war.
➕ A6 ✉ 9 Fuxing Lu, Haidian District ☎ 6851 4441 🕐 8:30–5 🚍 1, 4, 57 ♿ None 💷 Cheap

MUSEUM OF CHINESE HISTORY

Sharing a building with the Museum of the Chinese Revolution (► 43), the exhibits here become progressively more interesting as their coverage moves closer to modern times. Unfortunately, they are not explained in English. Check with the Museum for special exhibitions.
➕ H7 ✉ Tian'anmen Square, Dongcheng District ☎ 6512 8986 🕐 Tue–Sun 8:30–4:30 (last ticket 3:30) 🚇 Qianmen ♿ None 💷 Cheap

XU BEIHONG MEMORIAL HALL

Relatively unknown in the West, Xu Beihong (1895–1953) is China's foremost modern artist. The galleries contain many of his paintings, including ones of galloping horses for which he is most famous. Reproductions are on sale in the museum shop.
➕ E2 ✉ 53 Xinjiekoubei Dajie, Xicheng District ☎ 6225 2265 🕐 Tue–Sun 9–12, 1–5 🚇 Jishuitan ♿ None 💷 Cheap

Xu Beihong

The Shanghai artist Xu Beihong (1895–1953) experienced dreadful poverty after he was left as a teenager with the task of looking after his family when his father died. Later he travelled to France and became interested in the avant-garde but he never lost his interest in depicting Chinese life, and his political radicalism ensured his fame.

Xu Beihong is renowned for his paintings of horses

TEMPLES, CHURCHES & MOSQUES

See Top 25 Sights for
GREAT BELL TEMPLE (► 26)
IMPERIAL VAULT OF HEAVEN (► 45)
TEMPLE OF CONFUCIUS (► 46)
LAMA TEMPLE (YONGHEGONG) (► 47)

Religion

Taoism, Buddhism and Confucianism are the three main belief systems of Chinese religion. The government professes atheism and, while the freedom to practise religion is tolerated, there is strict control over places of worship (any new place of worship requires government approval) and contact with religious organisations outside China is not allowed. Mosques and Christian churches in Beijing also meet the needs of the city's worshippers.

BAIYUNGUAN TEMPLE

This Taoist temple, whose name means 'White Cloud', dates back to the Tang dynasty. A factory during the Cultural Revolution, it has been restored and is now busy with Taoist priests and worshippers. The temple decorations include many familiar Taoist symbols like the Linghzi mushrooms, cranes and storks. A giant ancient coin on show is one of the highlights.

➕ C7 ✉ 6 Baiyunguan Jie, Xibianmenwai, Xuanwu District ☎ 6346 3887 🕐 8:30–4:30 🚇 Fuxingmen 🚻 None 💷 Cheap

BEITANG (NORTHERN CATHEDRAL)

Built towards the end of the 19th century, the church – like many places of worship both Christian and non-Christian – was turned into a factory during the Cultural Revolution. Repair work was completed in the 1980s.

➕ F4/5 ✉ 33 Xishiku Dajie, Xicheng District ☎ 6617 5198 🕐 Services in Chinese Mon–Sat 6–8AM, Sun 6–9:30AM and 6–7:30PM 🚌 38, 47 🚻 None

Above: the Fayuansi Temple

FAYUANSI TEMPLE

This delightful Buddhist temple, with its six lilac-decked courtyards, is now a college for novice monks, whose earnest, saffron-robed figures can be seen at their studies. The first temple on this site was founded in 645, and earlier buildings served many purposes, including that of an examination hall. Look for the display of illustrated moralising texts on the right side as you go through the hallway leading to the main temple building.

➕ E9 ✉ 7 Fayuansiqian Jie, Xuanwu District ☎ 6353 4171 🕐 8:30–11, 2–4 (closed on Wed) 🚌 61, 109 🚻 None 💷 Cheap

GUANGJISI TEMPLE

A busy, functioning Buddhist temple redolent of incense, visited by a constant stream of devout worshippers. See it as part of a walk in this area of Beijing (► 16).

➕ E4/5 ✉ 25 Fuchengmennei Dajie, Xicheng District ☎ 6616 0907 🕐 8–4 🍴 ► 16 🚇 Fuchengmen 🚻 None 💷 Free

NANTANG CATHEDRAL (SOUTHERN CATHEDRAL/ ST MARY'S CHURCH)

Catholicism came to Beijing in the 17th century when Jesuit scholars were welcomed for their scientific, and specifically astronomical, knowledge. Nantang Cathedral is built on the spot where the most famous of these Jesuits, Matteo Ricci, lived.

🚇 E7 ✉ Xuanwumendong Dajie, Xuanwu District ☎ 6602 5221
🕐 Services in Latin Mon–Fri 6AM, Sat 6:30AM, Sun 7AM; service in English Sun 10AM 🚇 Xuanwumen ♿ None

Interior of South Cathedral

NIUJIE MOSQUE

The Chinese-style façade resembles that of a temple, but this is the largest mosque in Beijing – and the oldest founded in the late 10th century. Non-Muslims are allowed into the courtyard, but not the central prayer hall, where there are tombs of Muslim missionaries to China during the Yuan dynasty (1206–1368). The tower was used for observing the moon and calculating the time of Ramadan.

🚇 D9 ✉ Niu Jie, Xuanwu District ☎ 6353 2564 🕐 8–5 🚌 6
♿ None 💰 Cheap

WHITE DAGOBA (WHITE PAGODA) TEMPLE

It is not easy to miss this 45m-high pagoda, the largest in Beijing, built in the 13th century as a showpiece of the new Mongol capital. It was closed down and used as a factory in the Cultural Revolution. Nepalese influence in its construction is still apparent, and should survive the major renovation that was planned to be completed in 1999.

🚇 D4 ✉ Fuchengmennei Dajie, Xicheng District ☎ 6616 0211
🕐 9–4:30 🚇 Fuchengmen ♿ None 💰 Cheap

WUTA (FIVE-PAGODA) TEMPLE

Established in the 15th century, this little-visited Indian-style temple and its adjoining Museum of Stone Carvings (► 54) are well worth combining with a trip to the zoo (► 60). Standing behind two ancient ginkgo trees, the temple's pagodas are covered with exquisite Buddhist bas-relief; climb the stairway for a closer view. After being looted by Anglo-French troops around the turn of this century, the temple fell into obscurity.

🚇 B2 ✉ 24 Wutasicun, Haidian District ☎ 6217 3836 🕐 8:30–4:30 🍴 Nearby restaurant (Food St ► 62) 🚇 Xizhimen 💰 Cheap

Islam in China

There are many mosques in the city and the Niujie Mosque is on the main street of Beijing's Muslim community. Islam was first introduced into China in the Tang dynasty (7th–10th centuries) and is now the religion of various minorities, including the Hui (from western China), some of whom live in Beijing.

White Dagoba in Beihai Park

AREAS TO EXPLORE ON FOOT

Pavement stalls in Dazhalan Jie

The first hamburger

The eastern corner of the south end of Wangfujing Dajie, where it meets Dongchang'an Jie (➕ H7), was the prestigious site of China's first McDonald's. In 1994 the government aired the notion of closing it down for redevelopment purposes. McDonald's resisted, and the media turned it into an international news story. Victory for the government? The fast-food restaurant has now closed down. Victory for McDonald's? There are now more than 30 franchised clones across the city.

BAIWANZHUANGXI LU

This street, south of the zoo (➤ 60), is the Beijing home to the Turkic Uighur (pronounced wee-gar) community, usually resident in north-western China. Make a late evening visit when the restaurants and street stalls are open.

➕ A4 🍴 Shish kebabs, spicy mutton and nan bread (£) at most restaurants 🚇 Fuchengmen ♿ None

DAZHALAN JIE

Head south down Qianmen Dajie from Qianmen underground station and keep on the right side; after a string of stalls look for a blue-glassed building on the corner and 'Billy's Shop' across the road. Turn right down the pedestrianised *hutong* (➤ 19) here. Down the first alley on the left is a centuries-old pickle shop, while back down Dazhalan Jie are musty old department stores with grand architectural façades, and an ancient medicine shop. Look on the right for the arched entrance (red lanterns outside) of a famous old fabric store. This is a side of Beijing that is fast disappearing.

➕ G8 🍴 Fast-food place at Zhengyangmen (Qianmen Gate) (£) 🚇 Qianmen

QIANMEN DAJIE

During imperial times, shops and places of entertainment for common people were not allowed inside the walls of the Forbidden City, so the area south of Zhengyangmen (Qianmen Gate) developed into a hive of commercial activity, the legacy of which is still evident. It is especially popular with visitors from the provinces, and is an excellent area for foreign visitors to experience a colourful slice of

Chinese street life. Qianmen Dajie, the main street running south from Qianmen Gate, bustles with working-class Beijingers. Attractions include a famous vegetarian restaurant, the Gongdelin, at No 158 (► 64), fascinating side-streets like Dazhalan Jie (see opposite), and the Natural History Museum (► 54).

➕ G8 🍴 Fast-food places (£) and restaurants (£–££) 🚇 Qianmen

SANLITUN LU

Don't miss this street in the north-east of the city, in an area populated by embassies; it has an almost Mediterranean character that's not Chinese at all. One side of the street is filled with clothing stalls (► 75), the other with alfresco restaurants. Black-market traders offer pirated computer and music CDs. Popular with locals, expatriates and tourists.

➕ M3 🍴 Plenty of cafés and restaurants (£–££) 🚌 115, 118

XIDAN

The main thoroughfare that runs straight across the city from east to west changes its name four times and as Xichang'an Jie runs west from Tian'anmen Square before changing its name again to Fuxingmennei Dajie at Xidan. The Xidan area is worth exploring for its atmosphere, especially in the evenings when lively street stalls mushroom and crowds frantically shop for everyday household items.

➕ E6 ✉ Niu Jie, Xuanwu District
☎ 6353 2564 🕐 9–10PM
🚇 Xidan

WANGFUJING DAJIE

Once named Morrison St, after a London *Times* correspondent who lived at No 88, this is one of Beijing's most famous streets. A large part of its eastern side has been extensively redeveloped as a showcase of modern Chinese consumerism (► 76), but it is still an interesting walk (► 18) and a good place to observe Beijing's *nouveaux riches* at play.

➕ H5/6 🍴 From fast food (£) to fine dining in hotels (££–£££)
🚌 104, 211

City Views

The Palace View bar, on the 10th floor of the Grand Hotel (➕ H6) is an excellent place for views of the Forbidden City. The transmission tower for Central China Television also provides a spectacular view of Beijing from 240m above the ground (➕ west of A5 ✉ 11 Xisanhuanzhong Lu ☎ 6843 7755, ext. 377 🍴 Restaurant and coffee shop at the top).

Beijing's popular Silk Market attracts locals as well as tourists

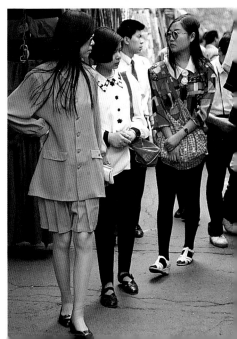

ATTRACTIONS FOR CHILDREN

See Top 25 Sights for
GREAT BELL TEMPLE (► 26)
SUMMER PALACE (► 24)
TIAN'ANMEN SQUARE (► 38)

Playgrounds

Most public parks have a playground suitable for toddlers and children below the age of ten, and some of the mechanical contraptions offer fun rides. Zizhuyuan (Purple Bamboo Park) (► 53) is good for rides; boat trips are also available here. Older children might enjoy the video arcade in the basement of the Jing Guang Hotel (➕ N5 ✉ Jing Guang Centre, Hujialou, Chaoyang District).

BEIJING AMUSEMENT PARK
Here in the south-west of the city, on the west side of Longtan Lake Park, is an impressive range of fun rides: ferris wheel, roller-coaster, waterslide, boat rides and shooting arcades.
➕ K10 ✉ Longtan Park, Chongwen District ☎ 6701 1155 🕐 9–6 🚌 60, 116 from Chongwenmen Dajie 🔥 None 💰 Expensive (but most rides included)

BEIJING ZOO
Although fairly depressing, the zoo is worthwhile for its famous giant panda house. Spare a moment for the lesser panda from Sichuan province, in a cage to the west of the main panda dwelling. The zoo is tucked away in the north-west of the city but easily reached by underground. A visit to the Museum of Stone Carvings (► 54) helps make the trip worthwhile.
➕ B3 ✉ Xizhimenwai Dajie, Xicheng District ☎ 6831 4411 🕐 8:30–5:30 (avoid weekends) 🍴 Nearby restaurant (Food Street ► 62) 🚇 Xizhimen 🔥 None 💰 Cheap

CHINA AVIATION MUSEUM
Military and civilian aircraft here include a twin-engined plane that Mao Zedong used for trips within China and the plane that flew over Tian'anmen Square on 1 October 1949. A separate building displays planes spanning the century.
➕ Off the map ✉ Xiaotangshan, Changping County ☎ 6178 4882 🕐 8–5 🚌 912 from Andingmen underground station, 345 🔥 None 💰 Cheap

CHINESE ETHNIC CULTURE PARK
Though most Chinese are Han people, there are still over 50 minority ethnic groups. In this park near the Olympic Sports Centre, exhibitions of architecture and the performing arts showcase the culture of diverse other groups. Wedding ceremonies, sports and song and dance performances also take place.
➕ Off the map ✉ Corner of Fourth Ring Rd and Beichen Lu ☎ 6206 3640/6206 3646 🕐 8:30–6PM 🍴 Food centre in the park 🚌 380, 407 🔥 None 💰 Expensive

MOVIE TOURIST CITY
A genuine film studio with sections set aside for visitors, including a horror set and children's games – the most popular game is laser tag.
➕ Off the map ✉ Corner of Third Ring Rd and Xitucheng 🕐 9–4 🚌 302, 375, 367 🔥 None 💰 Moderate

Youngsters enjoying a ride at Longtan Amusement Park

BEIJING
where to...

NORTHERN CHINESE CUISINE

Prices

The restaurant descriptions use symbols to show approximate prices, for a meal for two excluding drinks, as follows:

£ under 100 yuan

££ between 100 and 200 yuan

£££ over 200 yuan

Northern cuisine

This category of Chinese food – taking in the whole area north of the Yangtze – includes imperial cuisine (reserved for, and specially prepared for, the court), Beijing duck and traditional city fare, along with food from remote northern areas like Mongolia and Dongebi. Noodles and steamed bread provide the basic sustenance, instead of rice, accompanied by vegetables and cold appetisers. From the far north come hearty beef and lamb dishes.

BANPO PRIMITIVE HOT POT BEER HUT (£–££)

The primitive décor (bare walls and neolithic tools hanging from the ceiling) is a bit of a novelty – Banpo is the name of a neolithic village unearthed in the west of China – but the location is very accessible. Spend an enjoyable evening here tucking into the Mongolian hot pot meals, washed down by economically priced drinks.

✚ H5 ✉ 26 Wangfujing Dajie, Dongcheng District ☎ 6525 5583 ⏰ 11AM–1AM 🚌 103, 104, 108, 111

BEIJING EXPRESS (£)

An inexpensive place to enjoy northern Chinese street cuisine in comfortable and clean surroundings. The menu is divided into sections offering noodles, snacks, hot dishes and cold dishes: why not try a dish from each category? The noodle soup with double boiled spare ribs is recommended, as are the sautéed wild vegetables with shredded pork.

✚ A3 ✉ New Century Hotel, Shoudu Tiyuguannan, Haidian District ☎ 6849 2001 ⏰ Lunch and dinner 🚇 Xizhimen

BIANYIFANG ROAST DUCK RESTAURANT (££)

This famous roast duck restaurant has two dining areas, the first one pricier but also more pleasant, with more comfortable seats, than the second.

✚ J7 ✉ 2 Chongwenmenwai Dajie, Chongwen District ☎ 6712 0505 ⏰ Lunch and dinner 🚇 Chongwenmen

FANGSHAN (£££)

Court recipes once reserved for emperors' 19th-century mealtimes form the basis of the elaborate imperial cuisine served at this renowned restaurant in Beihai Park. Top marks for imperial-style surroundings.

✚ G5 ✉ Beihai Gongyuan (inside the east gate of Beihai Park) ☎ 6401 1879 ⏰ Lunch and dinner 🚌 13, 101, 103, 107, 109, 111

FOOD ST (£–££)

Situated behind the Xiyuan Hotel, close to the zoo, this is an excellent place to try standard northern Chinese cuisine at affordable prices. There are varied fresh fish dishes, noodles with shredded chicken, sweet dumplings, and delicacies like deep-fried scorpions. The barbecued meat cooked over charcoal and served on skewers is recommended.

✚ A3 ✉ Sanlihe Lu, Xicheng District ☎ 6831 3388 ⏰ Lunch and dinner 🚇 Xizhimen

GOLD CAT JIAOZI CITY (£)

An English menu lists many tasty versions of stuffed dumplings – the speciality here. Dine outside in spring and summer for an altogether enjoyable experience.

✚ N5 ✉ Tuanjiehu Gongyuan East Gate, Chaoyang District ☎ 6598 5011 ⏰ 11AM–6AM 🚌 302, 402, 405, 801

LI FAMILY RESTAURANT (£££)

The founder of this most highly regarded restaurant was the great grand-daughter of an employee in the Qing court who obtained the menus for Empress Dowager Cixi's meals. The tiny restaurant, part of a family home, serves imperial dishes accompanied by a small number of Beijing and Li family dishes.

➕ F3 ✉ 11 Yangfang Hutong, Deshengmennei Dajie, Xicheng District ☎ 6618 0107 🕐 Dinner (reservations up to two weeks in advance are necessary) 🚇 Jishuitan

QUAN JUDE KAOYADIAN (££–£££))

The name means 'old Duck', but don't be put off: this is a fine place for a Beijing duck banquet. The restaurant has been in the same family for nearly 150 years and is now the flagship for a group of restaurants in the city, including the takeaway outlet next door, offering the same, good quality dishes.

➕ G8 ✉ Qianmen Dajie, Chongwen District ☎ 6511 2418 🕐 Lunch and dinner 🚇 Qianmen

SI HE XUAN (££)

Black-and-white photographs of old Beijing adorn the walls, in the spirit of the traditional cuisine of the city, in which this restaurant excels. Lunchtime is the best value with cold appetisers like celery with tofu and hot dumplings, stuffed buns and noodles or congee (soupy rice); Chinese tea and pastries filled with lotus root complete a good meal.

➕ M7 ✉ Jinglun Hotel, 3 Jianguomenwai Dajie, Chaoyang District ☎ 6500 2266 🕐 Lunch and dinner 🚌 1, 4, 37, 52

TINGLIGUAN (££)

Dining rooms of the Tingliguan ('Pavilion for Listening to the Orioles') surround a courtyard in the Summer Palace (➤ 24). You'll find a clever mix of imperial cuisine and Cantonese dishes that appeal to the Western palate. Try the fresh fish, including carp, from nearby Kunming Lake.

➕ Off the map 12km north-west of the city centre ✉ Yiheyuan, Haidian District ☎ 6288 1955 🕐 Lunch and dinner 🚌 301, 303, 332, 333, 346, 384, 904

TUAN JIE HU BEIJING ROAST DUCK (££)

One of the most economical and visitor-friendly restaurants offering a good Peking duck. There are also lots of seafood dishes, as well as offerings that are less familiar to Western palates – like sautéed turtle.

➕ N5 ✉ Bldg. 3 Tuanjiehu Lu, Chaoyang District ☎ 6507 2892 🕐 Lunch and dinner 🚌 302, 402, 405, 801

Duck...and more duck

Slices of roast duck are placed inside a thin pancake along with onion or cucumber and sometimes sweetened with plum sauce or a wheat jam. The taste is very rich and it is best not to think about the cholesterol count. A real feast begins with cold duck and ends with duck soup. A side plate of mashed garlic acts as an antidote to the rich, oily duck skin and meat.

Alcohol

Alcohol is routinely served in restaurants in Beijing, but wine and spirits are only likely to be found in places catering for tourists. Beer is usually available in most establishments.

OTHER CHINESE CUISINE

Southern cuisine

'Everything with legs except a table, everything in the air except an aeroplane and everything under the sea except a submarine.' This Cantonese joke gives a fair idea of the variety of ingredients that go into southern cuisine. Fish – typically placed in a wok and cooked through light frying intially but mostly through steaming – is a special favourite, as are the sweet and savoury small plates that go by the name of *dim sum*, eaten for breakfast or lunch.

Sichuan

Outside China, Cantonese food may be the most widely known regional cuisine, but the western province of Sichuan provides the most surprises to the taste buds. The cunning use of spices, especially red chilli, gives Sichuan food a reputation for being very hot, but it is also very subtle. A typical starter might be fine slices of beef infused with the tangy peel of the kumquat.

AFANTI (££)

Roasted lamb or chicken with nan bread are favourites at this conveniently located Muslim Uighur restaurant. Ethnic music and dancing in the evening make for an enjoyable night out.
✚ K5 ✉ 2 Houguaibang Hutong, Chaoyangmennei Dajie, Chaoyang District ☎ 6525 1071 🕐 11AM until the last customers leave 🚌 101, 110, 202

CHAIRMAN MAO'S FAMILY RESTAURANT (££)

This restaurant is devoted to food from Hunan, Mao's province. Pork with bamboo shoots, a favourite dish of the Chairman, is always on the menu along with a number of typically hot dishes.
✚ J1 ✉ A4 Hepingli Zhongjie, Dongcheng District ☎ 6421 9340 🕐 Lunch and dinner 🚇 Yonghegong

CHAO YANG XIN JING (££)

This Cantonese restaurant serves a range of seafood and, though well off the tourist track, has an English-language menu. In summer the outdoor tables are crowded with contented diners until the small hours.
✚ Off the map, east of N6 ✉ 11 Hongmiao Lu, Chaoyang District ☎ 6502 3327 🕐 6AM–3AM 🚌 101, 112

DING TAI ZHEN (£)

The large menu in English features many fish dishes, and old-fashioned western favourites like chicken rice with ginger,

as well as unusual appetisers like lotus root. This licensed restaurant is suitable for vegetarians and is good for an inexpensive meal. Try the Iron Fairy tea. A word from the wise – avoid the loos!
✚ J5 ✉ 116 Dongsinan Dajie, Chaoyang District ☎ 6525 7578 🚌 110, 116, 120, 204

DYNASTY (££–£££)

Four dishes from the *dim sum* menu here make a good lunch for two: sautéed rice rolls, barbecued pork with raisin, deep-fried spring rolls, and dumplings with shark's fin soup are favourites. Ask which sauces go with each dish.
✚ N5 ✉ Jing Guang New World Hotel, Jing Guang Centre, Hujialou, Chaoyang District ☎ 6501 8888 🕐 Lunch and dinner 🚌 9, 113, 402, 405, 801

GONGDELIN (££)

This is a branch of a famous Shanghai vegetarian restaurant, with its own delightful English-language menu featuring, for example, 'chicken cutlets in the shape of lantern' and 'the Fire is singeing the Snow-Capped Mountains'. The food is excellent and the mock-meat dishes satisfy carnivores as well as vegetarians.
✚ G9 ✉ 158 Qianmen Dajie, Chongwen District ☎ 6511 2542 🕐 10:30 8:30PM 🚇 Qianmen

SICHUAN RESTAURANT (££)

Overlooks the lobby of

the Xiyuan Hotel. Be sure to try the Eight Treasures tea or the hotel's own strong brew of Kaiser beer. Spiced chicken is a fine cold appetiser and braised fish in black bean sauce a typical main course. The fried walnut makes a delicious dessert.

🔼 B3 ✉ Xiyuan Hotel, 1 Sanlihe Lu, Haidian District ☎ 6831 3388 🕐 Lunch and dinner 🚇 Xizhimen

SUI YUAN (£££)

Superb Cantonese cuisine in the Beijing Hilton. Specialities change, but you can rely on the stir-fried fish dishes, and in winter the Mongolian-style chicken and beef satay is unbeatable. A Beijing duck set menu is available, and at lunchtime the shrimp dumplings and spring rolls are tempting. Live classical music at night.

🔼 N2 ✉ Hilton Hotel, 1 Dongfang Lu, Dongsanhuanbei Lu, Chaoyang District ☎ 6466 2288 🕐 Lunch and dinner 🚌 302, 402, 801

TIANSHI (£–££)

Excellent and attractive vegetarian restaurant with 'mock meat' dishes like deep fried chicken, rice with seafood, braised eel. Superb non-alcoholic cocktails, beer and champagne. Pictures of famous vegetarians – Shakespeare? – line the stairs. Snacks and soft drinks are served downstairs.

🔼 J5 ✉ 57 Dengshikouxi Jie, Dongcheng District ☎ 6524 2349/6524 2476 🕐 8AM–midnight 🚌 108, 111

TIBET SHAMBALA (£)

The only Tibetan restaurant in Beijing (run by a Tibetan scholar) is well worth the rather long journey from the city centre. Meals start with yak butter tea and the dishes include wonderful noodles, barbecued lamb and a host of tastes unique to Tibetan cuisine.

🔼 A1 ✉ 301 Minzu Shipin Yitiaojie. Weigongcun Lu, Haidian District ☎ 6842 2631 🕐 Lunch and dinner 🚌 320, 337, 904

WISDOM BIRD (£–££)

Don't be put off by menu items like stewed bullfrog: alternatives include spare ribs with bamboo shoots and interesting fish dishes. Few tourists find their way to this restaurant, tucked away some 200m down a lane and not named in English.

🔼 Off the map, just north of A1 ✉ On the right side of a small lane leading off Baishiqiao Lu opposite the Friendship Hotel ☎ 6217 1941 🕐 11–10 🚇 Xizhimen

YU XIAN (£)

The chef and owner of this small restaurant was once Mao Zedong's chef; Mao's children and Deng Xiaoping have eaten here. The food consists of local items and traditional dishes from Hunan. Try the fishballs, or the meat-filled rolls that you fit into little pancakes before eating them.

🔼 H5 ✉ Cuihua Hutong, off Wangfujing Dajie, Dongcheng District ☎ 6524 5322 🕐 Lunch and dinner 🚌 103, 104, 108, 111

Eight Treasures tea

A speciality of Sichuan restaurants is Eight Treasures tea, served out of the longest teapot you are ever likely to see. The eight ingredients are: jasmine, jujube, walnut, fruit of Chinese wolfberry, raisin, crystal sherry, ginseng, and dried longan pulp. The taste is slightly spicy, and prepares you for the spicy flavours to come.

ASIAN RESTAURANTS

Asian food

Not so many years ago, the possibility of enjoying an authentic Indian or Thai meal in Beijing would have been unthinkable. Today, chefs are regularly brought in from other parts of Asia, and authentic pineapple fried rice, spicy Thai soup, nan bread, Masala tea and tandoori chicken offer exciting alternatives to Chinese food.

ASIAN STAR (££)

Eclectic menu featuring Thai, Malaysian and Indonesian fare as well as a host of Indian ones – thanks to an Indian chef, options such as curries and tandoori chicken vie with the Malaysian dishes as some of the best Asian eating you will find in Beijing.

✚ N4 ⊠ 26 Dongsanhuanbei Lu, Chaoyang District ☎ 6591 6716 🕔 Lunch and dinner 🚍 113, 402, 405

BOROM PIMAN (£££)

The consensus among Beijing's expatriate community is that this restaurant in the Holiday Inn out on the road to the airport offers the best Thai food in the city. The service is exemplary and the décor Thai.

✚ Off the map near the airport ⊠ Holiday Inn Lido, Jichang Lu, Jiangtai Lu, Chaoyang District ☎ 6437 6688 🕔 Lunch and dinner 🚍 401, 403

HEPINGMEN KOREAN BBQ (£–££)

Korean restaurants in Beijing tend not to translate their menus, so non-Korean diners must rely on photographs or look around to see what is being served. The speciality is barbecued meats: a small grill is brought to the table for diners to do their own barbecuing. Good fun for newcomers to Korean cuisine as well as for old hands – but not for those who dislike hot, spicy food.

✚ G8 ⊠ 15 Hepingmenwaidong Jjie, Chongwen District ☎ 6301 3117 🕔 Lunch and dinner 🚇 Hepingmen

OMAR KHAYYAM (££–£££)

Up-market prices, but authentic Indian cuisine for both vegetarians and meat-eaters. The menu is large enough to suit most tastes, and the lassi drinks are exellent. At weekends a reservation is recommended.

✚ L6 ⊠ Asia Pacific Building, 8 Yabao Lu, Chaoyang District ☎ 6513 9988 🕔 Lunch and dinner 🚇 Jianguomen

RASA SAYANG (££)

This restaurant offers the best selection of basic Indonesian dishes in town.

✚ Off the map ⊠ Holiday Inn Lido, Jichang Lu, Jiangtai Lu, Chaoyang District ☎ 6437 6688 🕔 Lunch and dinner 🚍 401, 403

RED BASIL (££–£££)

An excellent Thai restaurant. The menu does not indicate how spicy the various dishes are but the staff are helpful. The superb food prepared by Thai chefs warrants the trip to the Third Ring Road just south of Sanyan Bridge.

✚ N1 ⊠ Building 8, Nanxiaojie, Sanyuanli, Chaoyang District ☎ 6460 2339 🕔 Lunch and dinner 🚍 302

SAIGON INN (£££)

This restaurant in the Gloria Plaza Hotel serves traditional Vietnamese appetisers like *cha gio* and *goi cuon* (spring rolls), which you wrap up in lettuce and rice paper respectively. Tasty main dishes include chicken curry accompanied by shrimp salad, pickled vegetables and asparagus and crabmeat soup. The décor, right down to the chopsticks is Vietnamese, and traditional Vietnamese music plays softly in the background.

✚ L7 ✉ 2 Jianguomenwai Dajie, Chaoyang District ☎ 6515 8855 🕐 Lunch and dinner 🚇 Jianguomen

SANSI LANG (£–££)

The most affordable Japanese restaurant in the city offering good value for money. Try the tempura and sushi and, even though the menu is not in English, there are photographs of all the dishes.

✚ N2 ✉ 52 Liangmaqiao Lu, Chaoyang District ☎ 6464 5030 🕐 11–11 🚌 9, 300, 402, 801

SAWASDEE RESTAURANT (£££)

A Thai restaurant offering dishes like spring rolls and *tom yam* soup, *galng ka-ree* (yellow chicken) curry with potatoes and *kaow oh sup-pa-ros* (fried rice with pineapple and seafood). Most of the dishes are quite mild, so this is a good place to try Thai food if you're wary of too much spice.

✚ J5 ✉ Song He Hotel, 88 Dengshixikou Dajie, Dongcheng District ☎ 6513 8822 🕐 Lunch and dinner 🚌 104, 108

SHAMIANA (££–£££)

This was the first Indian restaurant to open in Beijing and it continues to provide quality meals prepared by an Indian chef. Some dishes may seem bland to connoisseurs but the chef will happily add more spice on request.

✚ D4 ✉ Holiday Inn Downtown, 98 Beilishi Lu, Xicheng District ☎ 6833 8822 🕐 Lunch and dinner 🚇 Fuchengmen

SUSAN'S CAFÉ (£)

An unpretentious, friendly little place opposite the Kempinski Hotel. Meat and vegetable curries of varying degrees of spiciness are the main dishes but soups and salads are also available. Cocktails are served (happy hour 3–6 daily).

✚ N2 ✉ Liangmaqiao Lu, Chaoyang District ☎ 6464 0930 🕐 11AM–2AM 🚌 9, 300, 402, 801

THAILAND EMPRESS SEAFOOD (££)

Reasonably priced Thai establishment with an emphasis on seafood but a good range of other dishes as well. The menu carries explanations in English.

✚ F5 ✉ Xihuangchenggennan Jie, Xicheng District ☎ 6617 5754 🕐 Lunch and dinner 🚌 22, 103

Quenching thirst

The Sawasdee Thai restaurant serves Guinness as well as other alcoholic drinks but for many diners a bottle of cold mineral water, readily available in all Beijing restaurants, serves as a better complement to hot and spicy food. Best of all is a platter of fresh fruit, a lassi drink from India or a glass of Thai iced coffee.

WESTERN RESTAURANTS

Dining with a view

On the 26th floor of the Xiyuan Hotel, the Carousel revolving restaurant serves Beijing and other Asian dishes (£££) while taking in panoramic views of the city. The TV Tower (➤ 59) has a restaurant and café but its view cannot match that of the Belle Vue restaurant on the 29th floor at the Kunlon Hotel (✚ N2 opposite the Lufthansa Centre, ➤ 76) which takes about 90 minutes to complete one revolution.

BEIJING AUTUMN JADE (££–£££)

A mixed menu of French, German and Russian dishes – steak, chicken Kiev and pork chops, for example – served in an elegant setting, accompanied by candlelight in the evening. Seafood dishes are also served.
✚ J6 ⊠ 3 Jinyu Hutong, Dongcheng District ☎ 6512 8833 ⏰ Lunch and dinner 🚌 104, 106

CAFE KRANZLER (££–£££)

Situated on the ground floor of the Lufthansa Centre, with tables looking out through plate-glass windows to the street, this comes to life in the evening, when live music helps provide a more relaxing atmosphere than might have seemed possible in this busy location. Steaks, pasta and pizza are on the menu.
✚ N2 ⊠ Lufthansa Centre, 50 Liangmaqiao Lu, Chaoyang District ☎ 6465 3388 ⏰ Lunch and dinner (closes 2AM) 🚌 9, 300, 402, 801

HOF BRAUHAUS (££–£££)

House specialities include Wiener schnitzel and smoked pork loin with sauerkraut and potatoes. The bonus is Hof Brauhaus' own beer, brewed using German technology. The menu is in English and German.
✚ N4 ⊠ 15 Dongsanhuanbei Lu, Chaoyang District ☎ 6591 4598 ⏰ 11:30AM– midnight 🚌 113, 117, 801

LAXENOXEN (££–£££)

For fresh Norwegian salmon you can't beat this Scandinavian restaurant in the Radisson SAS Hotel in the north-east of the city (➤ 84). Beef is regularly flown in, and the Sunday brunch is luxurious.
✚ Just north of M1 ⊠ 6A Beisanhuandong Lu, Chaoyang District ☎ 6466 3388 ⏰ Lunch and dinner 🚌 302, 379

LE PETIT PARIS (££)

A spacious French restaurant, complete with a reproduction of the bottom half of the Eiffel Tower, with a menu in French and English and a decent wine list. Crêpes here make a good lunch when you're shopping at nearby Sanlitun (➤ 75).
✚ M4 ⊠ 8 Gongrentiyuchangbei Lu, Chaoyang District ☎ 6507 2228 ⏰ 11AM–midnight 🚌 113, 117

LOUIE'S SPACE (£)

A modest little café opposite the Kempinski Hotel, serving steaks, salads and sandwiches. Open until 2AM. Happy hour from early afternoon until 8PM.
✚ N2 ⊠ Liangmaqiao Lu, Chaoyang District ☎ 6462 1973 ⏰ 11AM–2AM 🚌 300, 402, 801

MEXICAN WAVE (££–£££)

Margaritas and beer imported from Mexico, are an appropriate prelude to the pizzas, quesadillas, burritos, burgers and huge salads. Near the corner with Guanghua Lu.

🔳 M6 ✉ Dongdaqiao Lu, Chaoyang District ☎ 6506 3961 ⏰ 10ᴀᴍ–2ᴀᴍ 🚌 28, 403

MOSCOW (£–££)
For decades after it opened, in 1954, this Russian restaurant was prestigious. The reason to come here is the fun of dining surrounded by faded elegance, under chandeliers and amid fluted columns. While the spicy borscht is still worth ordering, some dishes can be disappointing. Try the steak with mushroom sauce or the chicken curry drumsticks.
🔳 C3 ✉ 135 Xizhimenwai Dajie, Xicheng District (access by a small road on the west side of the Beijing Exhibition Centre; look for *Mockba Pectopah* about 100m down on the right) ☎ 6831 6677 ext.4331 ⏰ Lunch and dinner 🚇 Xizhimen

POWER HOUSE (££)
Photographs on the menu here offer standard items like spaghetti bolognese, pork chops and burgers. Live music at night keeps things lively. Close to the Sanlitun area.
🔳 N4 ✉ Gongrentiyuchangbei Lu (opposite the Zhao Long Hotel), Chaoyang District ☎ 6462 9192 ⏰ 10ᴀᴍ–2ᴀᴍ 🚌 113, 117

ROMA RISTORANTE ITALIANO (£££)
Leather upholstery and wood panelling at this restaurant in the Palace Hotel (➤ 84) help create an elegant setting. Dishes from northern Italy, complemented by wines from a fine list. The set-

price Sunday brunch offers a lavish choice of appetisers, pastas, soups, salads and desserts.
🔳 J6 ✉ Jinyu Hutong, Dongcheng District ☎ 6512 8899 ⏰ Lunch and dinner 🚌 103, 104, 110, 116, 120

SYMPHONY (£££)
The period European dining room here is elegant and luxurious and the steaks and seafood are imported.
🔳 N2 ✉ Kempinski Hotel, Lufthansa Centre, 50 Liangmaqiao Lu, Chaoyang District ☎ 6465 3388 ⏰ Lunch and dinner 🚌 300, 402, 801

SZENARIO (££–£££)
At this delightfully informal Italian restaurant, start with the antipasto buffet, followed by pasta, pizza, salad or a grill.
🔳 L4 ✉ Swissotel (Hong Kong Macau Centre), Dongsishi Tiao Lu, Chaoyang District ☎ 6501 2288 ⏰ Lunch and dinner 🚇 Dongsishitao

TED'S CAFÉ (££)
Places serving both Chinese and Western dishes are not common; the pub-like Ted's Café is an honourable exception. Typical European meals are served after 9ᴘᴍ while hotter Sichuan fare is available for lunch or evening meal between 6 and 9. Live music at weekends, organised games of darts every Thursday.
🔳 M6 ✉ 58 Guandongdiannan Jie, Chaoyang District ☎ 6506 0329 ⏰ 24 hours 🚌 9, 113, 402, 405, 801

Fast food
Nearly all major franchised fast-food restaurants are adding outlets in and around Beijing: A&W, Baskin Robbins, Dunkin' Donuts, KFC, McDonald's, Pizza Hut and TGI Friday's. A stretch of Jianguomenwai Dajie (L7), the area around Zhengyangmen (Qianmen Gate ➤ 42) and Wangfujing (➤ 59) are the places to find out how American fast food translates in a decidedly Chinese setting.

ANTIQUES

Exporting antiques

Chinese authorities classify any item made before 1949 as an antique. The export of any such item must be approved by the Beijing Cultural Relics Bureau. Approval takes the form of a red wax seal and an official receipt; any genuine antique dealer should be able to show you this. As the vast majority of 'antiques' are really reproductions the need for export approval does not arise very often. If you buy an antique that lacks the seal, you can have it verified and approved at the Friendship Store (☎ 6401 4608 for an appointment) every Monday afternoon.

BEIJING CURIO CITY

This large mall has over 200 stalls selling a wide range of items from bric-à-brac to genuine antiques. The best time to visit is on Sunday morning, when vendors set up shop in the surrounding streets.

✚ Off the map, south-west of the city ✉ Dongsanhuan Nan Lu, west of Huawei Bridge ☎ 6773 6098 🕐 9–5

CHAOYANGMENWAI MARKET

Two large warehouses at the end of a small lane are stuffed with antique objects of desire: medicine cabinets, chests, first-class reproductions of Qing and Ming furniture, ceramics, Mao memorabilia, jewellery and other knick-knacks. A visit is vital for anyone thinking of buying a piece of furniture or a quality *objet d'art*. Packing and shipping are easily arranged. Serious bargaining is essential: try to end up paying less than half the price first quoted.

✚ L5 ✉ Shichangie, Chaoyangmenwai Dajie, Chaoyang District 🕐 9–6 🚇 Chaoyangmen

HONGQIAO MARKET

Seek out the antique shops on the third floor – easy to miss, tucked away behind the pearl stalls (► 73). A lot of the merchandise is reproduction, but some of the furniture is small enough to be portable and the temple plaques are appealing. Shop No 6 specialises in old clocks. Bear in mind when bargaining that these shops cater for tourists.

✚ J9 ✉ Tiantan Lu, Chongwen District 🕐 9–6 🚌 36, 39, 43

HUAXIA ARTS & CRAFTS BRANCH SHOP

The second floor of this government shop retails clocks, pocket watches, rugs, chinaware and woodcarvings from temples. Most of them are probably fake, but they look authentic.

✚ H6 ✉ 293 Wangfujing Dajie, Chaoyang District ☎ 6513 6204 🕐 9–7

LIANGMAHE MARKET

In an arcade opposite the Kempinski Hotel some 50 small shops sell pottery, paintings, old watches and antique furniture. One or two of the furniture dealers have a larger stock in their warehouses and will happily take potential customers there to view. However, there is a high mark-up, and only serious bargaining will result in a reasonable price.

✚ N2 ✉ 49 Liangmaqiao Lu, Chaoyang District ☎ 6501 3525 🕐 9–9 🚌 9, 300, 402, 801

LIULICHANG

Conveniently located south-west of Qianmen, this famous old street – recently renovated to look its age – is well worth a visit even if you buy nothing. Quality antique shops stock woodblock print reproductions, porcelain, jade, snuff bottles, paintings and a very few genuine antique pieces. Worth considering are the rubbings of bas-relief carvings taken off ancient temples and tombs. A number of the larger stores are government-owned; bargaining in this area is limited compared to the privately owned sector.

✚ F8 ✉ Liulichangdong Jie, Xuanwu District ⏰ 9–6 🚇 Qianmen

PANJIAYUAN MARKET

Come here on weekends, especially Sundays, early in the morning because after midday this market is already winding down. Most of the 'antiques' are fake but they are quality fakes and gratifying purchases may be made if you bargain rigorously. Never pay anything like the first price quoted. It is best to arrive by taxi, but make sure the taxi driver doesn't just drop you by the stalls selling worthless bric-à-brac – ask your hotel to specify in writing where you should go.

✚ M10 ✉ Huawei Lu Dajie, Dongsanhuan, Chaoyang District ⏰ 8–1 🚌 35, 41

QIANMEN CARPET

Wares at this establishment are similar to those at Xu Cai Chun (▶ below). There are some very expensive antique carpets from Xinjiang and Tibet as well as hand-made imitations and Henan silk carpets – the objectives of most visitors. The showroom is a converted air-raid shelter dating from the 1960s.

✚ K9 ✉ 44 Xingfu Dajie, Chongwen District ☎ 6715 1687 ⏰ 9:30–5:30 🚌 6, 35, 51, 60

TIANJIN

Serious antiques shoppers might consider a weekend excursion to Tianjin (▶ 20–1), where the antiques market takes over a part of Shenyang Dao in the centre of town. Sunday morning from 8 to midday is the best time. Close to the first exit of the expressway from Beijing to Tianjin is the well-established Ming and Qing dynasty antique furniture store, C L Ma Furniture Co (☎ 022–2933 5555).

✚ Off the map, about 80km east of Beijing 🚌 Buses from Beijing railway station

VAMBER ANTIQUE & ARTS HOUSE

This shop, part private enterprise and part government-owned, declares that it specialises in 'artificial antiques' – fakes at affordable prices, including some decent bronze and porcelain pieces. Packing and shipping can be arranged.

✚ G5 ✉ 29 Wusi Dajie, Dongcheng District ☎ 6401 0048 ⏰ Mon–Sat 9–7:30 🚌 103, 112

XU CAI CHUN

Claiming to be the largest antique carpet dealer in Beijing, this store retails hand-made reproductions of antique carpets from Tibet, Mongolia and other exotic corners of China. Expect to pay around 500 yuan per sq m. Credit cards are accepted here.

✚ Off the map ✉ Off Xiao Hong Men Rd (south of the Third Ring Road) ☎ 6764 3063 ⏰ 9–6

Cloisonné

Cloisonné is an attractive, colourful enamel finish applied to many types of decorative ware such as lamps, vases, incense burners, tea-sets, lanterns, tables, stools, prize cups and various silver-based items. It is produced by welding flattened wire on to a copper backing to form an outline. Enamel of different colours is then used to fill the outlined spaces with a range of rich shades, The Ming dynasty (1368–1644) was the heyday of cloisonné ware, but it remains popular today, and much modern work is based on traditional designs.

ARTS & CRAFTS

Ceramics

The history of ceramics in China is as old as the civilisation itself. The technology and art of design evolved from neolithic times, through the Bronze Age and all the great dynasties from the 6th century onwards. The Ming dynasty produced some of the most beautiful work through the use of under-glaze blue and white painting.

Old Peking

Two books first written in the 1930s by foreigners living in the city provide an insight into the old capital and its way of life. They are *Peking*, by Juliet Bredon and *In Search of Old Peking*, by Arlington & Lewisohn (both published by Oxford University Press). *Twilight in the Forbidden City*, written by Reginald Johnston, English tutor and tennis coach to the last emperor, Puyi, has also been republished by Oxford University Press.

ARTS & CRAFT SHOP

This shop in the prestigious World Trade Centre retails fine china, carpets and an array of expensive *objets d'art*, and has its own foreign exchange counter.
✚ N7 ✉ 1 Jianguomenwai Dajie, Chaoyang District ☎ 6505 2261 🕐 9:20AM–9:40PM 🚌 1, 4, 37

BEIJING JADE CARVING FACTORY

The wide selection of jadeware here ranges from magnificently ponderous examples of this renowned Chinese handicraft to the more luggage-friendly in size. Look carefully at some of the quality items, noticing how cleverly the differing shades of green are used in the design.
✚ L9 ✉ 11 Guangming Lu, Chongwen District ☎ 6702 7371 🕐 9–5

CUI WEN GE ART SEALS SHOP

Chops (▶ panel opposite), made from a variety of materials and to suit most budgets, are the speciality here. If you would like to have your name carved in Chinese, ask your hotel staff to write down the correct characters for you.
✚ F8 ✉ Liulichangdong Jie 🕐 9–5 🚇 Hepingmen

EAST GALLERY

A small selection of mostly contemporary paintings, plus some old photographs at reasonable prices. There are a couple of similar shops close by.
✚ M3 ✉ 28 Sanlitun Lu,

Chaoyang District ☎ 6415 7314 🕐 10–7 🚌 115, 118

FORBIDDEN CITY SHOPS

Small shops inside the Forbidden City include a stall at the entrance to the Gate of Supreme Harmony that sells an inexpensive and attractive poster map of the palace complex. The most useful gift shop, simply called Gift Shop, just inside the north gate (where the hired audiotapes are returned), has a small but discriminating selection of art books, quality reproductions of Ming and Qing art, CDs, puzzles, theme umbrellas and other souvenirs. Next door, the bookshop with the grandiose title Books of Cultural Relics, Archaeology & Arts has the city's best selection of translated academic titles on Chinese art and archaeology. Other arts and crafts shops form a shopping corridor where you can find affordable gifts such as painted perfume bottles.
✚ G5 ✉ Jingshanqian Jie, Dongcheng District 🕐 8:30–5 🚇 Qianmen

FRIENDSHIP JEWELLERY SHOP

Hardly anyone finds this place unless visiting the Ancient Observatory or arriving on a tour bus. The two floors are filled with display cabinets of gold and silver jewellery and precious stones.
✚ K7 ✉ 2 Beijing Guguang Xiangtainei, Jianguomen Dajie ☎ 6527 4012 🕐 9:30–6 🚇 Jianguomen 🚌 1, 4, 52

FRIENDSHIP STORE

Before the government abolished the Foreign Exchange Certificate (FEC) system in 1995, foreign visitors had to use FEC for the purchase of anything important. The Friendship Store was then the major shopping venue for visitors; Chinese citizens were not even allowed inside. The store remains well worth a visit, if only to check the fixed prices and the range of items. There are four levels; all but the second floor, where there is a foreign-exchange facility at a branch of the Bank of China, offer a good range of arts and crafts: jade, porcelain, cloisonné, lacquerware, silk, linen, paintings, carpets, works of calligraphy, and kites.

➕ L7 ✉ 17 Jianguomenwai Dajie, Chaoyang District ☎ 6500 3311 ⏰ 9–8:30PM 🚌 1, 2, 3, 4, 9, 802

HONGQIAO MARKET

The central area on the third floor is devoted to freshwater pearls. They hang by the hundreds from strings, and are made up on the spot to suit the customer's wishes. There are no fixed prices so bargaining is required. Experts can sometimes be seen rubbing two pearls together. The rougher the contact the better; if they rub together smoothly this suggests poorer quality. Arts and crafts shops share the same floor; some (Nos 213–14 and 218) specialise in cloisonné (➤ 71); shop No 219 is devoted to finely crafted gilded-silver ornaments. Another area is devoted to antiques (➤ 70).

➕ J9 ✉ Tiantan Lu, Chongwen District ⏰ 9–6 🚌 36, 39, 43

HONGSHENG MUSICAL INSTRUMENTS

The sign for this store is not in English but it is easy to locate on the west side of Wangfujing. As well as guitars and small brass instruments there is a selection of traditional Chinese instruments – not easy to find outside China.

➕ H6 ✉ 225 Wangfujing Dajie, Dongcheng District ☎ 6513 5190 ⏰ 9–6:30 🚌 104, 103, 803

LUFTHANSA CENTRE

The fifth floor of this large shopping plaza is devoted to arts and crafts and offers a wide choice of jade, pottery and porcelain and assorted collectables. A separate room serves as a gallery for Chinese prints. Prices are fixed but a 10 per cent discount is still worth trying for.

➕ N2 ✉ 50 Liangmaqiao Lu, Chaoyang District ☎ 6465 1188 ⏰ 9–9 🚌 300, 402, 801

SCROLL ALLEY

Although way off the beaten track, this motley street market is easy to reach by underground. Walk east from Chegongzhuang station, turning north when you see the stalls on your left. A good place to have pictures mounted as scrolls.

➕ D3/4 ✉ North of Ping'anlixi Dajie ⏰ 9–5 🚇 Chegongzhuang

Chops

Name chops – personalised stamps – have been used for thousands of years in China and, despite mass literacy, are still commonly used. In a number of official situations, where the West would demand a signature, the Chinese will stamp a document with their personal name chop. The chops are made of a variety of materials, marble, jade, wood and even plastic, and the better arts and crafts shops will stock a range to choose from. It is easy to have your name put on one in Chinese characters or in your own language. When making a purchase be sure to get an ink pad and ink; red has always been the traditional colour.

CLOTHING

Bargaining

In Sanlitun and the Silk Market there are no fixed prices, and bargaining is the rule. In general, try to bring down the vendor's first asking price before committing yourself to an offer and remember that you will always need to settle at a price above your first offer. A pair of Armani jeans should go for around 100 yuan, Caterpillar boots or a Gore-Tex jacket for around twice that.

ERMENEGILDO ZEGNA

This exclusive designer-clothing boutique is typical of the shops in the top-class Palace Hotel; its neighbours include Versace and Boss. The prices are often higher than those in Europe but wealthy Chinese customers have been known to turn up here with suitcases stuffed with cash and blow huge sums on a only a few garments.

✚ J6 ✉ Jinyu Hutong, Dongcheng District ☎ 6512 8899 ⏰ 10:30–9:30 🚌 110, 116, 120, 204

FRIENDSHIP STORE

You'll find clothing on the second floor. There is a terrific choice of silk, sold by the metre, and the selection of traditional Chinese dress is worth a look. It is a good idea to come here and check the quality and fixed prices before trying your hand at bargaining in the street markets.

✚ L7 ✉ 17 Jianguomenwai Dajie, Chaoyang District ☎ 6500 3311 ⏰ 9–8:30PM 🚌 1, 2, 3, 4, 9, 802

GANJIAKOU

This market attracts few tourists because the clothes are entirely Asian in style, but it will appeal to those interested in investigating the latest fashions from Taiwan and Korea. Stalls line the road, Sanlihe Lu, as far as Daiwanzhuangxi Lu. Bargaining is essential.

✚ B4 ✉ Sanlihe Lu, Haidian District ⏰ 9–5 🚌 102, 103, 114

HUFANG LU

This street market of busy stalls has a fast turnover of clothes but European or North American visitors may well find most of the garments unfashionable but prices are reasonable and occasionally worthwhile silk items turn up. Bargaining is essential.

✚ F8 ✉ Hufang Lu, Xuanwu District ⏰ 9–5 🚌 6, 14, 15

MILITARY SUPPLIES

This place, not far from the Jing Guang Centre, stocks garments and gear of the People's Liberation Army (PLA), including heavy-duty, double-breasted coats with gold buttons and PLA caps, complete with red star.

✚ N6 ✉ 23 Dongsanhuanbei Lu, Chaoyang District ⏰ 9–5:30 🚌 9, 13, 117, 350, 402, 405, 801

RUIFUXIANG SILK AND CLOTH STORE

The areas around Dazhalan Jie (➤ 58) – a hive of commercial activity for five centuries – is home to a number of interesting old stores, including the well-known Ruifuxiang, with its distinctive arched entrance and its façade decorated with storks. Raw silk is the main draw here, in a dazzling choice of colours, textures and patterns.

✚ G8 ✉ 5 Dazhalan Jie, Xuanwu District ⏰ 9–8 🚇 Qianmen

RUSSIAN MARKET

This is the unofficial name for the clothing market that starts half-way up

Ritan Lu and continues round the corner into Yabao Lu. Everything is geared towards the many Russian shoppers who arrive in Beijing on the Trans-Siberian railway with empty bags and return carrying or wearing as much as is humanly possible. Fur coats are a big draw – sable, mink, rabbit and fox – but there is also a fair selection of gloves, belts, scarves, women's garments and other assorted clothing items. The familiar designer names are not seen here and the styles may seem garish to European shoppers, but there are bargains to be had. However, the vendors like to sell in bulk and may ask how many identical items you are interested in.

✚ L6 ✉ Ritan Lu and Yabao Lu, Chaoyang District ⏰ 9–dusk 🚇 Jianguomen

SANLITUN LU

The Silk Market is by far the best known street for designer clothes but a visit to Sanlitun Lu (▶ 59) may well prove equally gratifying. As the stalls are mainly on one side of a street, there is more space for walking, looking and trying on. The atmosphere is less hectic than the Silk Market and, often, better prices can be negotiated. The bulk of the merchandise consists of designer-label jeans, shirts, and women's wear. A couple of stalls sell shoes and, at the far end where wicker furniture is sold, the shops continue

round the corner to a fruit and vegetable market.

✚ M3 ✉ Sanlitun Lu, Chaoyang District ⏰ 9–7 🚌 115, 118

SILK MARKET

A visit to this crowded market may convince you that very few visitors leave Beijing without having purchased a designer-label item of clothing or something in silk at a fraction of the shop price. Silk Market is a small lane, off the main road, crammed with stalls on both its sides. Shoppers, mostly visitors and expatriates, but some Beijingers too, fill every space and at times the atmosphere can seem frenzied. Apart from silk and cashmere, available at a fraction of their price in the West, bargains are to be had in Gore-Tex and down jackets as well as shirts, pullovers, raincoats, shoes and patchwork quilts. Famous brand names sit alongside impressive fakes and factory seconds: be on your guard, and always check for imperfections.

✚ M6/7 ✉ Xiushuidong Jie, Chaoyang District ⏰ 10–dusk 🚇 Jianguomen

YUANLONG SILK CORPORATION LTS

This is one of the oldest established silk stores in Beijing. A tailoring service is available. The store is easy to find since it is close to the north entrance of Tiantan Park.

✚ H9 ✉ Tiantan Lu, Chongwen District ☎ 6701 2854 ⏰ 9–5 🚌 34, 35, 36

Silk

Gorgeously embroidered silk shirts, blouses, underwear, trousers, pyjamas, bedspreads and gowns suggest themselves as ideal gifts. The Silk Market and the Friendship Store are both good hunting grounds, along with the large government-owned Beijing Silk Corporation, near the south gate of the Temple of Heaven. Bear in mind, though, that many items of silk clothing that seem such good value will never be the same after cleaning, even dry cleaning.

75

DEPARTMENT STORES & SHOPPING CENTRES

Shopping

Beijing's social revolution is nowhere more apparent than in the changed shopping scene. It is still possible to come across old state-owned stores whose surly staff give the clear impression that they don't want to be bothered by a troublesome customer with the audacity to wish to buy something. However, market forces are rapidly transforming everything, from the design of the store, inside and out, down to the new-minted smiles on the faces of helpful assistants. Most important, the shelves are now stocked with quality foreign-made goods and consumer items that were unknown a decade ago.

BEIJING DEPARTMENT STORE

It seems hard to believe that this store can survive for much longer in this prestigious location and in competition with Sun Dong An Plaza (➤ this page). A little more than 10 years ago this was Beijing's showpiece department store but now, upstaged by Beijing's newly arrived array of huge, smart shopping malls, its amateurish displays and general drabness puts it on a par with a cast-off statue of Lenin. See it while it lasts.

🚇 H6 ✉ 255 Wangfujing Dajie, Dongcheng District ☎ 6512 6677 🕐 8:30–8:30 🚌 104, 103

CHINA WORLD TRADE SHOPPING CENTRE

Chairman Mao would be appalled by this monument to yuppie consumerism. Among the chic boutiques and lifestyle stores is a well-stocked arts and craft shop (➤ 72), a useful deli, a drugstore and a large branch of the Hong Kong supermarket chain, Wellcome, which stocks an excellent range of local and Western foods.

🚇 N7 ✉ 1 Jianguomenwai Dajie, Chaoyang District ☎ 6505 2288 🕐 9–9 🚌 1, 4, 37, 52

CVIK SHOPPING CENTRE

Centrally located on Jianguomenwai Dajie and easily reached by subway, this up-market plaza is a Sino-Japanese joint venture with stores selling a wide range of imported merchandise. Fast-food outlets in the basement.

🚇 L7 ✉ 22 Jianguomenwai Dajie, Chaoyang District ☎ 6512 4488 🕐 9AM–9:30PM 🚇 Jianguomen

LUFTHANSA CENTRE

Very large with expensive produce, the centre has the advantage of housing one of Beijing's best supermarkets. A number of pleasant restaurants and cafés in the vicinity help sustain weary shoppers.

🚇 N2 ✉ 50 Liangmaqiao Lu, Chaoyang District ☎ 6465 1188 🕐 9–9 🚌 300, 402, 801

SUN DONG AN PLAZA

This is the big one, the glitzy flagship of the renowned and revamped Wangfujing. The 11-storey plaza with three basement levels opened in 1998. Its 120,000sq m of floor space includes department stores, clothing shops, an eight-screen cineplex, a food court, restaurants and an entertainment centre.

🚇 H5 ☎ 6527 6688 ✉ Wangfujing Dajie, Dongcheng District 🕐 9–9 🚌 104, 103

VANTONE NEW WORLD SHOPPING CENTRE

Easily reached by underground and close to an interesting part of town (➤ 16), this is a new, glossy, shopping mall. Many outlets from international companies.

🚇 D5 ✉ 2–8 Fuchengmenwai Dajie, Xicheng District ☎ 6858 8256 🕐 Mon–Thu 9–9; Fri–Sat 10–10 🚇 Fuchengmen

CURIOS, CARPETS & COMPUTERS

BEIJING MARCO POLO CARPET

This elegant shop deals in new, handwoven wool carpets and silk rugs in a pleasing variety of designs. Prices range from 2,400 to 88,000 yuan (try for a discount). Shipping can be arranged.

🔢 N7 ✉ L211, 2nd Floor, China World Tower, World Trade Centre, Jianguomenwai Dajie, Chaoyang District ☎ 6505 1974 🕐 9:30–9PM 🚌 1, 4, 37, 52

FOREIGN LANGUAGES BOOKSTORE

At one time this was Beijing's only store selling publications in English and other foreign languages. It still has the largest stock of such books in the city. As well as books and tapes in English and other languages, a range of dictionaries and other reference material is available in the Foreign Language Reference Bookstore at No 219 Wangfujing (entrance through the Dunkin' Donuts shop).

🔢 H6 ✉ 235 Wangfujing Dajie, Dongcheng District ☎ 6512 6922 🕐 9–8.30 (closes at 7PM in winter) 🚌 104, 211

SOUVENIR & BRIC-À-BRAC MARKET

A useful row of stalls near the Peace Hotel sells inexpensive Chinese gifts and mementoes which make good souvenirs. Copies of the *Little Red Book* are originals from the Cultural Revolution, while the glitzy watches and musical lighters bearing the face of Mao are newly made.

🔢 J6 ✉ Jinyu Hutong, Dongcheng District 🕐 10–dusk 🚌 104, 106

STAMP MARKET

Asian stamps – some rare, postcards and phone cards are on sale and there are usually some stalls dealing in coins, including the old bronze ones with holes in the middle.

🔢 Off the map ✉ Funite Furniture City, Beisihuanzhong Jie 🕐 9–5 🚌 302

TIANTAN PARK MARKET

A covered corridor near the park's east entrance is filled with stalls displaying bric-à-brac and cultural curios from the 1960s. Look out for the ubiquitous Maoist clocks depicting revolutionary peasants holding aloft the *Little Red Book*.

🔢 J9 ✉ East side of Tiantan Park, Chongwen District 🕐 9–5:30 🚌 6, 15, 17, 20, 35, 39, 43, 106

ZHONGGUANCUN

Computer shops are concentrated here in the north-west of the city. (From Xizhimen underground station take a minibus along Baishiqiao Lu.) You will see the shops a couple of stops past the Friendship Hotel. A wide range of software (beware – some is pirated), hardware and peripherals are available.

🔢 Off the map, north of A1 ✉ Haidian Jie, Haidian District 🕐 9–5 🚌 301, 303, 332, 333

Beijing books

The *Beijing Scene* guidebook (scene@well.com) is compiled by a group of expatriates (Beijing Scene Publishing, 400 Main St, Ansonia, CT 06401, USA) and is well worth dipping into for its wealth of informed and practical information. *The Forbidden City* by Mary Holdsworth and Caroline Courtauld (1995, Odyssey Press) is the most attractively produced book on its subject. *From Emperor to Citizen* (1987, Oxford University Press) is the autobiography of the last emperor, who lived in the Forbidden City until 1924. Good places to buy books on Beijing include the gift shops in the five-star hotels, notably the Swissotel (▶ 84), the Foreign Languages Bookstore (▶ this page) and two shops inside the north gate of the Forbidden City (▶ 72).

BARS & LICENSED CAFÉS

A fast-changing scene

Always call before heading off for the night – don't forget to ask your hotel to write down the name and address in Chinese for the benefit of taxi drivers. Beijing's licensed cafés, which function as informal restaurants during the day and early evening, gradually transform themselves into drinking bars as the night goes on.

ANNIE'S CAFÉ

'BYO' with a difference: you can bring your own food and prepare it for free in the kitchen. Few customers do, preferring to enjoy chatting over beers in this sociable sidewalk café/pub.

✚ M4 ✉ Sanlitun Lu, Chaoyang District ☎ 6594 2894 🕐 11AM–2AM 🚌 115, 118

BLUE HAND

This little bar opposite the Kempinski Hotel is frequented by expatriates and foreign students who value the inexpensive beer and food. On warm summer nights, the outdoor seating is an added attraction.

✚ N2 ✉ Liangmaqiao Lu, Chaoyang District 🕐 24 hours 🚌 300, 402, 801

CHAMPAGNE BAR

One of the better hotel bars in Beijing. The resident band, typically Filipino, jump-starts the evening around 7:30, after happy hour, and continues until 1AM. Reservations are available.

✚ N5 ✉ Jing Guang Centre, Dongsanhuanbei Lu, Chaoyang District ☎ 6501 8888 ext. 2561 🕐 4PM–1AM 🚌 112, 113, 9, 402

COCO CLUB

Latin American music and food sets the scene in this comfortable hotel bar on Wangfujing. Early in the evening you can enjoy a game of darts, or a quiet conversation may be enjoyed, but when the band starts up, just sit back and enjoy the show.

✚ H5 ☎ 6513 6666 ✉ Prime Hotel, 2 Wangfujing Dajie, Dongcheng District 🕐 6–1:30AM 🚌 104, 111

FRANK'S PLACE

One of the first bars in the Sanlitun area this remains a firm favourite with regulars. A good place to catch an international sports event on television.

✚ M4 ✉ Gongrentiyuchangdong Lu, Chaoyang District ☎ 6502 2617 🕐 11:30AM–1:30AM 🚌 120, 117

GOOSE & DUCK

A passable imitation of an English pub, with Bass ale from the barrel. There is an extensive menu of Asian and Western dishes and live music most nights.

✚ L6 ✉ 4 Ritanbei Lu, Chaoyang District ☎ 6509 3777 🕐 11AM–2AM 🚇 Jianguomen

HERE & NOW

A very small bar but easy to locate, being opposite the Workers' Gymnasium, and worth seeking out for its avant-garde arty atmosphere. When the place is not crowded the interior, which aspires to be a work of art, can be appreciated.

✚ L4 ✉ Gongrentiyuchangdong Lu, Chaoyang District ☎ 6416 0927 🕐 2PM–2AM 🚌 113

HOUSE BAR

Hard to know if this is a bar or just a licensed café. Either way it is worth a visit to sample the reasonable choice of drinks and the food menu offering an eclectic mix of American and Asian dishes.

➕ M6 ✉ Guanghua Lu, Chaoyang District ☎ 6595 2485 🕐 11AM–2AM 🚌 28, 34, 48, 403

JACK AND JILL BAR

This friendly pub is typical of the new breed of bar opening in the Sanlitun area. The décor is bright and cheerful and the staff anxious to please. A pleasant place to relax in the evening after a shopping trip.

➕ M3 ✉ 52 Sanlitun Lu, Chaoyang District ☎ 6416 4697 🕐 6PM–late 🚌 115, 118

JAZZ YA

One of the best cocktail menus in this part of town draws local yuppies and expatriates from around the globe. The food is Western, while the jazz is international.

➕ M4 ✉ 18 Sanlitun Lu, Chaoyang District ☎ 6415 1227 🕐 11AM–2AM 🚌 115, 118

JOHN BULL

Brass fittings, dark wood and memorabilia complement fish and chips and Yorkshire pudding in this mock-English pub. The first pub in Beijing to serve Guinness, John Bull, and Tetley's bitter on draft.

➕ L6 ✉ 44 Guanghua Lu, Chaoyang District ☎ 6532 5905 🕐 11AM–midnight 🚌 1, 4, 9, 802

MAGIC MUSHROOM

After a hectic twirl through the Silk Market

(➤ 75), this bar, conveniently located at the north end, offers a rest. At night a DJ often plays modern music to suit the style of the avant-garde interior.

➕ M6/7 ✉ Xiushudong Jie, Chaoyang District ☎ 6592 1446 🕐 6PM–2AM 🚇 Jianguomen

MINDER CAFÉ

All the basic ingredients for a good night out: decent pub food, live music, no cover, and a comfortable, spacious area to stretch your legs.

➕ M4 ✉ Nansanlitun, Chaoyang District ☎ 6500 6066 🕐 11:30AM–2:20AM 🚌 115

NASHVILLE

This country and-western bar has live music most nights – 'down-home' folks having a good time. Happy hour 5–8.

➕ M4 ✉ Dongdaqiaoxie Jie, Chaoyang District ☎ 6502 4201 🕐 2PM–2AM 🚌 115

OWL PUB

The main appeal of this upstairs bar is the large screen which shows a film daily at 8PM, just when the happy hour comes to an end. The draught beer is especially reasonably priced. The entrance is next to the City Hotel.

➕ M4 ✉ 4 Gongrentiyuchangdong Lu, Chaoyang District ☎ 6592 6290 🕐 11AM–3AM 🚌 115, 113

PUBLIC SPACE

With its buoyant décor, air of relaxed informality and tables out on the

Pub crawling

The Sanlitun Lu area is the only part of Beijing where you can pub-crawl on foot. In addition to the the establishments mentioned on these pages, there are a host of other places in the vicinity. The small *hutongs* between Gongrentiyuchangdong Lu and Nansanlitun Lu (➕ M4) are alight with neon at night and more bars cluster behind the Swing bar at No 58 further up Sanlitun Lu.

Beijing Internet

At the time of writing, the pioneering Keep in Touch bar (☎ 64625280), opposite the Kempinski Hotel (✚ N2), is the nearest Beijing gets to a cybercafé. Log in for a drink and an electronic chat (intouch@public3.bta.net.cn). Open from 5PM to around 1AM. Live music and displays of Beijing student art add to the modernist mood.

pavement, this typical Sanlitun bar is buoyantly decorated and stays open until dawn if demand warrants.
✚ M3 ✉ 50 Sanlitun Lu, Chaoyang District ☎ 6416 0759 ⏰ 11AM–3AM 🚌 115, 18

REDWOOD BAR

The main attractions are the pool table, the dart board, and the live country-and-western-style music.
✚ N4 ✉ Gongrentiyuchangbei Lu (opposite Zhao Long Hotel), Chaoyang District ☎ 6462 9143 ⏰ 6PM–3AM 🚌 113, 117

RICHMOND BREWERY

The Richmond Brewery at 46 Dongdanbei Dajie (✚ J6) is easy to find, being one block east of Wangfujing Dajie, but for atmosphere it is worth heading out to the north-west of the city to locate the second Richmond Brewery in Haidian, not far from Beijing University. The spacious bar is usually packed with students.
✚ Off the map, north of A1 ✉ 29 Haidian Lu, Haidian District ☎ 6523 1039 ⏰ 10AM–2AM 🚌 301, 303, 332

SAN FRANCISCO BREWING COMPANY

For many customers, the draw is the selection of six microbrews (including raspberry ale). You can sample them before moving on to pints or take-home mini-kegs. A large screen shows movies, accompanied by home-made sourdough bread and pizzas, and a decent selection of Cuban cigars.
✚ L4 ✉ West Wing, Beijing Asia Hotel, Xinzhong Jie, Chaoyang District ☎ 6500 7788 ⏰ 11:30AM–11:30PM 🚇 Dongsishitao

SCHILLER'S

This bar opposite the Kempinski Hotel has a reputation among the expatriate community and locals alike for friendly service and relaxed atmosphere. Food is served, and there are a few tables outdoors.
✚ N2 ✉ Liangmaqiao Lu, Chaoyang District ☎ 6461 9276 ⏰ 7AM–1AM 🚌 300, 402, 801

SHADOW CAFÉ

Out-of-centre bar in the student area of Haidian with surprisingly chic décor and jazz music. At weekends there is usually some kind of live musical entertainment.
✚ Off the map, north of A1 ✉ 31 Kexueyuan Nanlu, Haidian District ☎ 6261 8587 ⏰ 8.30PM–2AM 🚌 301, 303, 332

WATER HOLE

The long happy hour (3–7PM) draws a regular crowd. With a good selection of quick meals, many customers find little reason to move on during the course of an evening.
✚ M6 ✉ 3 Guanghua Lu, Chaoyang District ☎ 65074761 ⏰ 11AM–midnight 🚌 28, 43, 48, 403

Clubs & Discos

CD CAFÉ JAZZ CLUB
The archetypal jazz club, smoky and dim, where you can relax and observe the city from an outdoor patio. Live musicians appear at weekends (small cover).

➕ N3 ✉ Dongsanhuanbei Lu, Chaoyang District (south-west of Museum of Agriculture) ☎ 6501 8877 🕐 9:30AM–2AM (closed on Mon & Tue) 🚌 300, 402, 801

FREEZER DISCO
The best hotel disco in the city, with live bands.

➕ Off the map ✉ Holiday Inn Lido, Jichang Lu, Jiangtai Lu, Chaoyang District ☎ 6437 6688 🕐 8PM–2AM (3:30AM at weekends) 🚌 401, 403

HARD ROCK CAFÉ
Rock memorabilia, pricey drinks and tasty barbecued pork chops and grilled fajitas. A resident band plays short sessions after 9PM, except Sunday, there is a disco (cover).

➕ N2 ✉ 8 Dongsanhuanbei Lu, Chaoyang District (next to Great Wall Sheraton Hotel) ☎ 6590 6688 🕐 Sun–Thu 11:30–2, Fri–Sat 11:30–3, 🚌 300, 402, 801

NIGHTMAN DISCO
Only a few years ago, discos were unknown in China, so although the Nightman may seem a little unsophisticated, it is still remarkable how exuberantly Beijingers have warmed to discos.

➕ M1 ✉ 2 Xibahenan Lu (opposite west gate of International Exhibition Centre), Chaoyang District ☎ 6466 2562 🕐 8:30PM–2AM 🚌 302, 379, 18

POACHERS INN
Known for being rowdy; on weekends, after midnight, the place pulses with more energy than the average bar due to the loud pulsating rhythms of its heavy rock-type music. Revellers often arrive here after decamping from more staid venues. Cover charge on weekends.

➕ N5 ✉ West gate of Tuanjiehu Park, Dongsanhuanbei Lu, Chaoyang District ☎ 6532 3063 🕐 10PM–5AM 🚌 115

SAN WEI BOOKSTORE
The floor above the bookselling area is a teahouse by day and a buzzing bar at night. The décor is unusual but it suits the music, usually either live classical Chinese fare or laid-back jazz. Well worth a visit.

➕ E7 ✉ 60 Fuxingmennei Dajie, Xicheng District (opposite Minzu Hotel) ☎ 6601 3204 🕐 9:30AM–10:30PM 🚇 Fuxingmen

STORM BAR
This new bar in the north-east part of the city has a spacious dance floor, a discriminating bill of live bands, and balcony seating for those who prefer to watch. The local draft beer is reasonably priced.

➕ Just north of M1 ✉ Zuojiazhuangbeilishangye Lu, Chaoyang District ☎ 6464 8988 🕐 7PM–3AM 🚌 302, 379

Food, drink and culture
On Sunday mornings at the Jianguo Hotel (➕ M7) on Jianguomenwai Dajie a small classical orchestra provides a highbrow backdrop for a relaxing drink or meal. The atmosphere is pleasant, despite the setting in a hotel foyer, and if you feel like something a little louder, the adjoining Charlie's Bar is always a lively and sociable place.

ON STAGE

Acrobatics

The art of acrobatics – the physical feat and spectacle of gymnastic display – was practised in China over 2,000 years ago and is still going strong. Training academies enrol students of primary school age, and it is not uncommon to see very young children performing alongside seasoned professionals. Each troupe develops its own programme, blending vaudeville with gymnastics and acrobatics that require an incredible degree of training and concentration.

BEIJING CONCERT HALL

There is nowhere better to appreciate classical Chinese music than in the 1,000-seat Beijing Concert Hall, known for its excellent acoustics. Western music is also performed.

🔲 F7 ✉ 1 Beixinhua Jie, Xincheng District ☎ 6605 5812
🕐 Evenings 🚇 Xidan

CHANG FU GONG DINNER SHOW

On weekends the New Otani Hotel hosts an evening's entertainment of Chinese music, acrobatic displays, a traditional Chinese play and a buffet dinner featuring both Western and Chinese food, including roast duck.

🔲 L7 ✉ Hotel New Otani, Chang Fu Gong, 26 Jianguomenwai Dajie, Chaoyang District ☎ 6512 6106
🕐 7–9:30PM 🚇 Jianguomen

CHINA ACROBATIC TROUPE

This remarkable troupe, founded over forty years ago, offers one of Beijing's more enjoyable evening experiences. Their repertoire encompasses plate stacking and spinning, tightrope walking, magic and juggling, interspersed with breath-taking gymnastic displays that are often packed with dramatic surprises featuring bicycles or pieces of furniture. Highly recommended.

🔲 N5 ✉ Chaoyang Theatre, 36 Dongsanhuanbei Lu, Chaoyang District (opposite Jing Guang Hotel) ☎ 6507 2421
🕐 7:15PM 🚌 9, 113, 402, 405, 801

CHINA PUPPETRY THEATRE

Chinese shadow puppetry is a dying art, so an opportunity to see a show at the China Puppetry Theatre should not be missed, especially if a troupe from the countryside is performing.

🔲 Off the map ✉ A1, Anhuaxili, Chaoyang District (off Beisanhuan Xilu, the Third Ring Road, in the north of the city) ☎ 6424 3698 🕐 Sat 10:30AM & 3PM; Sun 3PM 🚌 300, 302

EXPERIMENTAL THEATRE FOR MODERN DRAMA

It is only since the demise of Mao's fourth wife, an actress and the notorious leader of the Gang of Four, that the authorities have encouraged non-Chinese forms of theatre. This hall is the main venue for such endeavours, and while some shows are in Chinese, international groups also perform in English.

🔲 G/H3 ✉ Mao'er Hutong, Xicheng District ☎ 6403 1009
🕐 Evenings 🚌 5, 107, 305

GLORIA SHOWCASE

A nightly show at the Gloria Plaza Hotel includes a roast duck dinner followed by magic, acrobatics, singing and traditional dancing.

🔲 L7 ✉ Gloria Plaza Hotel, 2 Jianguomenwai Dajie, Chaoyang District ☎ 6515 8855
🕐 Dinner 6:30, Show 7:30
🚇 Jianguomen

HUAXIA CULTURAL AND MARTIAL ARTS CENTRE

Different groups perform here on different nights of the week, perhaps staging a cultural narrative dance, like the traditional Chinese story of the Monkey King, or more often a display of martial arts. The Wushu, a fast and skilful performance of tai chi using swords, is a regular feature of the weekday evening shows.
🚇 H6 ✉ National Children's Arts Theatre, Dong'anmen Dajie, Dongchen District ☎ 6512 9687 🚌 103, 104

LAO SHE TEAHOUSE

The Chinese cultural shows staged here nightly enliven excerpts from Chinese opera with comedy routines (in Chinese but highly visual), martial arts displays, acrobatics, unicycling and magic.
🚇 G7 ✉ 3rd Floor, Da Wan Cha Building, 3 Qianmenxi Dajie, Xuanwu District ☎ 6303 6830 🕐 7:40–9:20 🚇 Qianmen

LIYUAN THEATRE

The Beijing Opera Troupe performs Chinese opera here daily. Screens alongside the stage carry English translations, and English programme notes help you to appreciate what is going on as you sit at the Ming-style tables sipping tea while enjoying the show.
🚇 F9 ✉ Qianmen Hotel, 175 Yong'an Lu, Xuanwu District ☎ 6301 6688 ext.8860 🕐 7:30–8:40 🚇 Qianmen

POLY PLAZA INTERNATIONAL THEATRE

This is a major venue for ballet, music and opera – Puccini's *Turandot*, the New York City Ballet or the Beijing Jazz Festival.
🚇 L4 ✉ 14 Dongzhimennan Dajie, Chaoyang District ☎ 6500 1188 ext.5682 🚇 Dongsishitiao

ZHENGYICI THEATRE

The history of this theatre goes back to 1620, when it was first built as a temple. Converted into a hotel after 1949, then finally closed down, it was saved from demolition in 1994 by a millionaire opera *aficionado* who financed a lavish reconstruction. Today, there is nowhere better to watch Beijing opera. Admission usually includes tea and biscuits (during the day, the theatre functions as a teahouse).
🚇 F7 ✉ 220 Xiheyan Dajie, Xuanwu District District ☎ 6318 9454 🕐 Nightly performances 🚇 Xuanwumen

ZHONGHE THEATRE

Though not such a magnificent theatre as the Zhengyici (➤ above), the Zhonghe is also responding to the revival of interest in Beijing opera and is arguably the best place to experience this unique art form. It is now a regular venue for performances.
🚇 G8 ✉ 5 Liangshidian Jie, Chongwen District ☎ 6303 7083 🕐 Evenings 🚇 Qianmen

Chinese opera

This highly stylised ancient art form has only a passing resemblance to Western opera and leaves most Westerners utterly bemused. The richly costumed players mix dance and song with mime – accompanied by Chinese instruments. Some grasp of the basic plot will help in understanding the action. The usual five-hour performance is reduced to a mere 90 minutes for the benefit of foreigners, although full performances are rare nowadays. The shortest performances are at the Lao She Teahouse (➤ this page).

LUXURY HOTELS

Room prices

Approximate prices for a double room:

Luxury   over 1500 yuan
Mid-range   700–1500 yuan
Budget   under 700 yuan

Use your hotel

Beijing hotels offer one invaluable service apart from providing a room and shelter: they will write down your destination in Chinese for you to show to taxi drivers when you go out. Ask the doorman to make sure that the driver knows exactly where you want to go – and don't forget to take the hotel's own namecard with you for the return journey.

CHINA WORLD

Consistently one of Beijing's best hotels for its over 700 tastefully furnished rooms, superb restaurants and first-class gym, swimming pool and golf centre with two golf simulators.

✚ N7 ✉ 1 Jianguomenwai Dajie, Chaoyang District ☎ 6505 2266; fax 6505 3167 🚍 1, 4, 37, 52

GREAT WALL SHERATON

In the Sanlitun diplomatic district, a short taxi ride from the city centre, on the Third Ring Road. Built around a seven-storey atrium loaded with creature comforts.

✚ N3 ✉ 10 Dongsanhuanbei Lu, Chaoyang District ☎ 6500 5566; fax 6500 1938 🚍 300, 402

HILTON

Over 300 rooms, convenient to the airport and the Sanlitun diplomatic and shopping district. Calm and attractive.

✚ N2 ✉ 1, Dongfang Lu, Chaoyang District ☎ 6466 2288; fax 6465 3052 🚍 300, 402, 801

NEW CENTURY

Good for families and sports-lovers. The recreation centre includes a good-size pool, a bowling alley and outdoor tennis courts. Good transportation to the city centre.

✚ A3 ✉ Shoudu Tiyuguannan Lu, Haidian District ☎ 6849 2001; fax 6849 1103 🚇 Xizhimen

PALACE

The Palace vies with the China World as Beijing's best hotel and exudes luxury with confidence. Over 500 luxury rooms, within walking distance of the Forbidden City. Attractions include Chinese and Western restaurants, a pool, a health club and a disco.

✚ J6 ✉ 8 Jinyu Hutong, Dongcheng District ☎ 6512 6192; fax 6512 7118; 🚍 103, 11, 106

RADISSON SAS

Terrific rooms, décor, a good-size pool, tennis and squash courts and a Finnish sauna help make the Radisson popular, especially with Scandinavians. A large supermarket is next door.

✚ Just north of M1 ✉ 6A Beisanhuandong Lu, Chaoyang District ☎ 6466 3388; fax 6465 3186 🚍 302, 18

SWISSOTEL

Few hotels in Beijing have geared themselves so successfully and pleasantly to the needs of Western holidaymakers. An underground station is nearby, and the facilities are generally excellent including those for visitors with disabilities. Airport shuttle bus, too.

✚ L4 ✉ Hong Kong Macau Centre, Gongshi Tiao Lu, Choyang District ☎ 6501 2506; fax 6849 1103 🚇 Dongsishitao

MID-RANGE HOTELS

HOLIDAY INN DOWNTOWN

One of three Holiday Inns in Beijing, this one is conveniently close to a underground station and shopping malls. It has a good recreation centre and an affordable Western-style restaurant.

✚ D4 ✉ 98 Beilishi Lu, Xicheng District ☎ 6833 8822; fax 6834 0696 🚇 Fuchengmen

MINZU

A good hotel in a useful location just west of the city centre. Over 600 recently renovated rooms, plus a gym and a billiards room.

✚ E7 ✉ 51 Fuxingmennei Dajie, Xicheng District ☎ 6601 4466; fax 6601 4849 🚇 Xidan

OCEAN

Located in an up-and-coming Chinese commercial area whose nightclubs come alive with neon at night, this smart modern hotel is within walking distance of the Forbidden City.

✚ J6 ✉ 189 Dongsinan Jie, Dongcheng District ☎ 6522 8888; fax 6522 9564 🚌 110, 116

OLYMPIC

This grey monolith is a smart modern hotel and has room rates that are almost in the budget category. The only drawback is the location. A bus ride and underground journey from the city centre.

✚ A2 ✉ 52 Baishiqiao Lu, Haidian District ☎ 6217 6688; fax 6217 4104 🚇 Xizhimen

PEACE

This quality hotel at the top end of the price range, is in the heart of the city, with over 500 rooms, an indoor swimming pool, and both Western and Chinese restaurants.

✚ J6 ✉ 3 Jinyu Hutong, Dongcheng District ☎ 6512 8833; fax 6512 6863 🚌 104, 111

SONG HE

Well versed in the art of dealing with Western visitors and situated conveniently close to Wangfujing Dajie and the Forbidden City. Room rates are at the top end of the category.

✚ J5 ✉ 88 Dengshikou Dajie, Dongcheng District ☎ 6513 8822; fax 6513 9088 🚌 111, 108

QIANMEN

Not too far from the Forbidden City, the Qianmen has a smart lobby, good restaurants, a gym, sauna and billiard room. Rates are at the lower end of the price category.

✚ F9 ✉ 175 Yong'an Lu, Xuanwu District ☎ 6301 6688; fax 6301 3883 🚌 15, 25, 102

XINDADU

Also called the Beijing Mandarin, this smart four-star hotel is in the north-west of the city, south of the zoo. It has a swimming pool, a sauna and fitness centre and several restaurants.

✚ B4 ✉ 21 Chegongzhuangxi Lu, Xicheng District ☎ 6831 9988; fax 6833 8507 🚇 Xizhimen

Rest assured

The days when hotel staff, regardless of the guest's disposition, casually strolled uninvited into hotel rooms to refill the hot water flasks are long gone. The general standard of hotels that welcome foreign guests is high. When you choose accommodation in Beijing today, a hotel's location and availability of transportation to the city centre are usually more relevant considerations than fear of unacceptable standards. (Apart from the Olympic and Xindadu, all the hotels on this page are close to the city centre.)

BUDGET ACCOMMODATION

Worth considering

Backpackers favour the Jinghua Hotel (☎ 6722 2211) on Nansanhuan Zhong Lu for its budget dormitory accommodation, inexpensive restaurants, economically-priced tours to the Great Wall, bicycle rental facility and general willingness to provide information. The big drawback is its location, on the southern end of the Third Ring Road. Take bus 17 from Qianmen to the Haihutun bus station and walk from there.

DONG FANG

Very good value for a hotel with this level of facilities. Located in the Qianmen area, the Dong Fang has eight restaurants, a sauna and gym, a business centre and a laundry. All 320 rooms are air-conditioned.

✚ F9 ✉ 11 Wanming Lu, Xuanwu District ☎ 6301 4466; fax 6304 4801 🚍 59, 105

FANGYUAN

Tucked away down a street off Wangfujing. Rooms are rather drab, but good value considering the central location.

✚ H5 ✉ 36 Dengshikouxi Jie, Dongcheng District ☎ 6525 6331 🚍 103, 104, 111

FAR EAST HOTEL

Affordable accommodation in the heart of the Dazhalan area, within walking distance of Tian'anmen Square. Has a Chinese restaurant.

✚ F8 ✉ 90 Tieshuxie Jie, Xuanwu District ☎ 6302 8811; fax 6301 8233 🚇 Qianmen

FEIXIA

Backpackers recommend its budget doubles (under 200 yuan). Rooms with shared facilities cost less.

✚ C7 ✉ Building 5, Xiabanmenwai Dajie, Xuanwu District ☎ 6301 2228; fax 6302 1764 🚇 Nanlishi Lu

GUO AN

A 128-room hotel with air-conditioning, in an accessible location close to the city centre and well served by buses. It also has a fast food restaurant – McDonald's.

✚ M5 ✉ 1 Guandongdianbei Jie, Chaoyang District ☎ 6500 7700; fax 6500 4568 🚍 109, 101, 110, 112

GUOTAI

The Guotai has a terrific location in the heart of the city and is favoured by visiting Russians, who are within walking distance of their favourite market (► 74). Lots of facilities, including a cash-only currency exchange and restaurants near by.

✚ M7 ✉ 12 Yonganxili, Jianguomenwai Dajie, Chaoyang District ☎ 6501 3366; fax 6501 3926 🚇 Jianguomen

GUOZHAN

This modern hotel is an affordable option for anyone seeking budget accommodation within reach of good food: the Laxenoxen restaurant of the Radisson SAS Hotel (► 68) and a huge super-market are across the road. The hotel has some 70 standard rooms with air-conditioning, and a Sichuan restaurant.

✚ Just north of M1 ✉ 10 Beisanhuandong Lu, Chaoyang District ☎ 6463 9922; fax 6467 9060; e-mail guozhan@public3.bta.net.cn 🚍 302, 379

RAINBOW

A decent modern Chinese hotel, with few foreign visitors and little English spoken, in the interesting Qianmen area. Restaurants include one offering medicinal cuisine and a Japanese restaurant.

✚ F9 ✉ 11 Xijing Lu, Xuanwu District ☎ 6301 2266; fax 6301 1366 🚍 59, 106, 343

BEIJING
travel facts

ARRIVING & DEPARTING

Before you go

- Visitors must hold a valid passport (with at least six months to run from the date of your planned visit to China) and a visa.
- A single-entry visa is usually valid for 30 days and must generally be used within three months of issue. Visas are available through your country's Chinese embassy or consulate and through specialist tour operators.
- One-month visa extensions can be arranged through the Public Security Bureau ✉ 85 Beichizi Dajie ☎ 6525 5486.
- No vaccinations are required but some doctors recommend inoculation against hepatitis A.

When to go

- The best time to visit is between September and mid-November followed by April and May.

Climate

- There are four distinct seasons with extremes of temperatures in winter and summer.
- Freezing winds from Siberia can drop the temperature to -20°C mid November to March.
- April and May are dry, with a wind from the Gobi Desert blowing across the city.
- From June to August it is uncomfortably hot (around 26°C), and very humid.
- The weeks between September and mid-November have pleasant temperatures and little rain.

Arriving by air

- Capital Airport is 25km north of Beijing.
- The taxi fare into the city is around 100 yuan.
- Shuttle buses run every half-hour

between the airport and the city. The fare is 16 yuan. There are two services, A and B, and between them they stop along the way near most of the big hotels. Tickets are purchased on the bus and a route leaflet is available from the airport information desk.

Arriving by train/bus

- There are five railway stations. The new West Railway Station at Lianhuachi (🚩 A8) handles routes to and from the south and west, including Hong Kong. There are no international bus routes, but four main stations serve buses to different parts of the country.

Customs regulations

- Authorisation is required for the export of antiques (► 70). Chinese currency cannot be exported. Two litres of any alcohol may be imported.

Departure/airport tax

- 90 yuan departure tax.

ESSENTIAL FACTS

Electricity

- Current is 220 volts. Beijing plugs come in a bewildering variety of sizes and types and though big hotels can supply adaptors it is best to bring your own.

Etiquette

- Confrontation or a public display of anger is counter-productive.
- Other public displays of strong emotion are not advisable.
- Avoid discussing Chinese domestic politics.

Insurance

- Travel insurance covering medical expenses is absolutely essential.
- In the event of illness or injury

requiring treatment, keep all your receipts in order to claim on your return home. Try to obtain an English translation of any documents/receipts written in Chinese.

Lone and women travellers
• Generally very safe.

Money matters
• RMB (Renminbi) is the currency of China and the basic unit is the yuan, which is made up of 10 jiao (pronounced as mao), each of which is again divided into 10 fen. There are paper notes for 1, 2, 5, 10, 50 and 100 yuan, and the smaller 1, 2 and 5 mao. There are also coins for 1, 2 and 5 yuan, 1, 2 and 5 mao, and 1, 2 and 5 fen.
• Most major credit cards are accepted at hotels, and the number of smarter restaurants and stores where you can use them is increasing all the time.
• Travellers' cheques are not only safer than cash, they also attract a better exchange rate. They can be cashed at branches of the Bank of China and at bureaux de change in hotels.
• As a rule, whenever prices are not displayed in writing, bargaining is probably expected. Politely ask for a discount. If the price still seems high, ask again. Bear in mind that once you make an offer, you will probably need to go above it eventually. Ask yourself whether the price difference you are bargaining over is really that much when converted to your own currency.

National holidays
• 1 Jan (New Year's Day)
• Chinese New Year/Spring Festival. This is governed by the lunar calendar and usually falls in late Jan or early Feb. Everything closes, so try to avoid this time.
• 8 Mar (International Working Women's Day)
• 1 May (International Labour Day)
• 4 May (Youth Day)
• 1 Jun (Children's Day)
• 1 Jul (Anniversary of Founding of Communist Party of China)
• 1 Aug (Anniversary of Founding of the PLA)
• 1 Oct (National Day)

Opening hours
• Banks and offices: Mon–Fri 9–5 (closed 1–2 hours for lunch).
• Shops: Generally 9–6, often later. Private shops stay open as demand warrants.

Places of worship
• Catholic: St Mary's Church Nantang Cathedral (Southern Cathedral) ✉ Xuanwumendong Dajie, Xuanwu District ☎ 6602 5221.
• Protestant: Beitang/Northern Cathedral ✉ 33 Xishiku Dajie, Xicheng District ☎ 6617 5198.
• Church of Jesus Christ of Latter-Day Saints ✉ Capital Mansions, 4th Floor, 6 Xinyuannan Lu, Chaoyang District ☎ 6532 4251.
• Judaism: Weekly Sabbath services ✉ Capital Mansions, 3rd Floor, Capital Club Athletic Centre, 6 Xinyuannan Lu, Chaoyang District ☎ 6512 6662/6505 3701.

Student travellers
• Generally, no discounts are available to student travellers.

Time difference
• Beijing is 8 hours ahead of Greenwich Mean Time. New York is 13 hours behind Beijing.

Tipping
• Tipping is not routinely expected, except for guides, who appreciate a small tip.

Toilets

- Hotels and better restaurants have Western-style toilets. Expect Asian-style hole-in-the-ground toilets (dip and pour as well as flush) elsewhere. Outside better hotels and restaurants, standards of cleanliness are not those of the West.

Tourist offices

- There is no tourist information office but a tourist hotline ☎ 6513 0828 is available. Hotel staff are usually helpful with everyday questions like how to get somewhere by bus, where to find the nearest supermarket and so on. If they are not too busy, they may also check on opening hours and the like (▶ panel on page 6).

Visitors with disabilities

- Little or no provision is made for visitors with disabilities. However, Beijing's broad, smooth streets are more user-friendly than those of most other Asian cities.
- Public transport is best avoided – the buses are overcrowded and jerky in motion.

PUBLIC TRANSPORT

How to use the underground

- The underground runs between 5AM and 10:30 or 11PM on two lines. The main circle line runs beneath the Second Ring Road; the second line, of less use to visitors, runs west from Xidan. A short walk is necessary to connect from one line to the other.
- Station names are in English on the platforms and an announcement in English is made on the train as it approaches a station. The only problem you may have is trying to work out in which

direction a train is heading when it pulls into the station where you are waiting.

How to use the buses

- There is a bewildering variety of vehicles: red and white, blue and white, trolley-buses, double-decker buses and private minibuses that carry the same number as the bus route they follow. On minibuses, you can always get a seat, and the vehicle will stop anywhere along the route. Public buses are often horrendously crowded in contrast and only the few air-conditioned ones – like bus 801, which runs between the Lufthansa Centre (🚌 N2) and the junction with Jianguomenwai Dajie (🚌 N7) – offer any comfort.
- Know your destination stop in Chinese – better still, have it written down.

Where to get maps

- The map that accompanies this book shows underground stations (in blue) and many bus routes (in red). Some hotel shops sell a Chinese/English city map that shows all the bus routes.

Types of ticket

- Underground tickets cost 2 yuan, regardless of the length of the journey, and are purchased inside the station.
- Bus tickets are calculated according to the length of the journey. The basic fare is 0.5 yuan and longer journeys cost 0.8 yuan. Tickets are purchased from the conductor but often the buses are so crowded that you have difficulty even seeing him! Fares on minibuses range between 3 and 6 yuan depending on length of journey.

Taxis

- Taxis are plentiful and inexpensive and, along with the underground, provide the best means of getting around. There are different types of taxi. The least expensive are small yellow vans which are less comfortable than a bus. Stick with the regular small car taxis, whose meters start at 10.4 yuan for the first 4km and then increase at 1.6 yuan per km, or the plusher sedan taxis whose meters start at 12 yuan and increase at 2 yuan per km. Always ask someone at your hotel to write down your destination in Chinese and show this to the driver before setting off. Also ask your hotel doorman to make sure the taxi driver knows where you're going.

MEDIA & COMMUNICATIONS

Sending letters and packages

- The easiest way to send letters and postcards is to let your hotel do it for you.
- Sending packages is time-consuming and often frustrating since printed matter has to be wrapped by postal officials. Leave them open because they must be inspected at the post office.
- Smaller packages can be sent from most post offices. Larger parcels need to go from the main post office – the International Post Office (➕ L6 ✉ Jianguomenbei Dajie).

Telephones

- Local calls are free, and hotels usually charge only a nominal fee at most.
- The easiest and least expensive way to make an international call is to use a card telephone in a hotel. Cards come in denominations of 10, 20, 50 and 100 yuan and may be purchased from hotel shops and hotel business centres.
- Use business centres in hotels to send faxes. It does not matter if you are not a guest.

Newspapers and magazines

- The only Chinese newspaper in English is the *China Daily*. It carries domestic and international news and is readily available in hotels. On Fridays, the *China Daily* carries entertainment listings as well as details of special food promotions.
- Foreign newspapers like the *International Herald Tribune* and magazines like *Time* and *Newsweek* are available in hotel shops. French and German newspapers and magazines are available in some top-class hotels.
- *Beijing this Month* is an official tourist magazine that carries current listings. It is available through hotels.

Television

- Better hotels carry CNN, as well as Star TV from Hong Kong, which has some English-language programming.
- Check the *China Daily* for the times of the short English-language news broadcasts on state television channels.

EMERGENCIES

Emergency phone numbers

- Emergency numbers are answered only in Chinese:
- Police: 110
- Ambulance: 120
- Fire: 119

Embassies and consulates

- Australia ✉ 21 Dongzhimenwai Dajie ☎ 6532 2331

91

- Canada ✉ 19 Dongzhimenwai Dajie ☎ 6532 3536
- France ✉ 3 Dongsanjie, Sanlitun ☎ 6532 1331
- Germany ✉ 5 Dongzhimenwai Dajie ☎ 6532 2161
- Ireland ✉ 3 Ritan Donglu ☎ 6532 2691
- Italy ✉ 2 Dong'erjie, Sanlitun ☎ 6532 2131
- New Zealand ✉ 1 Dong'erjie, Ritan Lu ☎ 6532 2731
- UK ✉ 11 Guanghua Lu ☎ 6532 1961
- USA ✉ 3 Xishui Beijie, Jianguomenwai Dajie ☎ 6532 3831

Medical treatment
- Better hotels have their own med-ical services. Contact them in the first instance. Clinics with English-speaking staff that treat foreigners include:
- Hong Kong International Medical Clinic ✉ Swissotel (Hong Kong Macau Centre), Dongsi TiaoLu, Chaoyang District ☎ 6501 2288
- International Medical Clinic ✉ Lufthansa Centre, Regus Office Building, Room 106, 50 Liangmaqiao Lu, Chaoyang District ☎ 6465 1561
- Sino-Japanese Friendship Hospital ✉ Yinghua Donglu, Hepingli Beikou ☎ 6422 1122 ext.3411

Medicines
- Shops in top-class hotels have their own shops that often sell a range of simple medicines – most notably the Watsons store at the Holiday Inn Lido, Shoudujichang Lu (outside the city centre, towards the airport). Some bigger supermarkets, like those in the Lufthansa Centre and the China World Trade Shopping Centre (► 76) are also worth trying. The International Medical Clinic (see above) has a pharmacy.

Sensible precautions
- Beijing is generally very safe.

- Pickpockets operate in crowded places like railway stations and on buses. Keep small cash at hand but always ensure your wallet or purse is secure.
- Leave money and important documents in your hotel room safe or safety-deposit box.
- Always keep travellers' cheques separate from your record of their numbers, and note the emergency contact number in case of loss.
- Bring with you a photocopy of your passport and visa and keep it separate from the original.

LANGUAGE

- In general, the better the hotel the better the standard of English spoken and understood. On the street, you cannot rely on commu-nicating in any language other than Chinese, although many people know a little English, it is useful (as well as courteous) to know some basic spoken Chinese.
- When setting out anywhere always ask the hotel to write down the place and address in Chinese and carry your hotel card with its address in Chinese for your return journey.
- Chinese characters are rendered into the Latin alphabet by the official system of Romanisation known as *pinyin*.
- The modern phonetic romanised form of Chinese is called 'pinyin'. It is largely pronounced as written, but note the following:
  a as in c*a*r
  c as in bi*ts* when an initial conso-nant
  e as in h*e*r
  i as in f*ee*t unless preceded by c, ch, r, s, sh, z, sh, when it becomes *er* as in her
  j as in *g*in
  o as in f*o*rd

q like the ch in *ch*in
s as in *s*imple
u as in oo in c*oo*l
w as in *w*ade, though pronounced by some as v
x like the sh in *sh*eep but with the s given greater emphasis
y as in *y*oyo
z as ds in li*ds*; zh as j in jam

Basics

yes	shi
no	bu shi
I don't understand	bu dong
Do you understand?	Dong ma?
when?	shenme shihou?
where?	nar?
telephone	dianhua
police	jingcha
toilet	ce suo
excuse me	dui bu qi
time	shijian
today	jin tian
tomorrow	ming tian
yesterday	zuo tian
morning	shang wu
evening	wan shang
afternoon	xia wu
left	zuo
right	you
south	nan
north	bei
east	dong
west	xi

Greetings, etc.

hello/how are you	ni hao
please	qing
thank you	xiexie
goodbye	zai jian
cheers!	gan bei
no problem	mei wen ti
I'm fine	wo hen hao
My surname is…	Wo xing…
I am from	Who shi…laide
Are you married?	Ni jiehunle ma?

Getting around

Where is…?	…zai nali?
taxi	chuzu che
airport	fei ji chang
train	huoche
bus	gong gong qi che
bicycle	xi xing che
ticket	piao
turn right	You zhuan
turn left	Zuo zhuan
I'm lost	Wo milule
hotel	fandian
room	fang jian
post office	youju
bank	yin hang

Medical

Doctor	yi sheng
Aspirin	zhitongpian
I'm sick	Wo sheng-bingle
hospital	yiyuan
pharmacy	yaodian

Shopping

how much?	Duo shao qian?
too expensive	tai gui le
a little cheaper	pian yi dian ba
gift	li wu
credit card	xin yong ka
postcards	ming xin pian
stamps	you piao
antique	guwu
silk	sichou
jade	yu
carpet	di tan
rice	mifan
beer	pijiu
coffee	ka fei

Numbers

0	ling	9	jiu
1	yi, yao	10	shi
2	er, liang	11	shiyi
3	san	12	shier
4	si	20	ershi
5	wu	21	ershiyi
6	liu	100	yibai
7	qi	200	erbai
8	ba	1000	yiqian

INDEX

CityPack
Beijing

Written by   Sean Sheehan
Edited, designed and produced by
   AA Publishing
Maps   © The Automobile Association 1999
Fold-out map © RV Reise- und Verkehrsverlag Munich · Stuttgart
   © Cartography: GeoData

Distributed in the United Kingdom by AA Publishing, Norfolk House, Priestley Road, Basingstoke, Hampshire, RG24 9NY.

The contents of this publication are believed correct at the time of printing. Nevertheless, the publishers cannot be held responsible for any errors or omissions or for changes in the details given in this guide or for the consequences of any reliance on the information provided by the same. Assessments of attractions, hotels, restaurants and so forth are based upon the author's own personal experience and, therefore, descriptions given in this guide necessarily contain an element of subjective opinion which may not reflect the publishers' opinion or dictate a reader's own experiences on another occasion.

We have tried to ensure accuracy in this guide, but things do change and we would be grateful if readers would advise us of any inaccuracies they may encounter.

Acknowledgements

Sean Sheehan would like to thank the following people in Beijing who helped with the research and writing of this guide: Rita Goh; Audrey Guo; Dennis Holmes; Veronica Ann Lee; Foued El Mabrouk; Greg Pringle; Zhang Qingyun; Li Tong; Phillipa Yule; Janet Zhang; Lin Zesheng.

The Automobile Association wishes to thank the following photographers, libraries and museum in the preparation of this book:
Art Directors & Trip Photo Library F/Cover main pic;
Ingrid Booz Morejohn/Picture Works 5a, 5b, 7, 8, 9, 11, 19, 20/1, 32b, 52, 53, 59;
Robert Harding Picture Library 32a;
Pictures Colour Library 28a, 28b;
Neil Sketchfield 15
Spectrum Colour Library F/Cover b, 18, 23a, 41a;
Xu Beihang Museum 55.
All remaining pictures were taken by Gordon Clements and are held in the Association's own Library (AA Photo Library) with the exception of the following pages: Ingrid Booz Morejohn F/Cover a, 12, 20, 23b, 29b, 30a, 61a; Alex Kouprianoff 6/7, 17, 27, 29a, 30b, 34b, 47b, 61b, 87a.

COPY EDITOR *Julia Cady* VERIFIERS *Accuracy Language Services, Beijing*
INDEXER *Marie Lorimer*

Titles in the CityPack series

- Amsterdam ● Atlanta ● Bangkok ● Barcelona ● Beijing ● Berlin ● Boston ●
- Brussels & Bruges ● Chicago ● Dublin● Florence ● Hong Kong ● Istanbul ●
- Lisbon ● London ● Los Angeles ● Madrid ● Miami ● Montréal ● Moscow ●
- Munich ● New York ● Paris ● Prague ● Rome ● San Francisco ● Seattle ●
- Singapore ● Shanghai ● Sydney ● Tokyo ● Toronto ● Venice ● Vienna ●
- Washington DC ●